Comedy, Chaos- and Cowboys!

The Red Dwarf Companion

By Joe Nazzaro

BearManor Media.com

Comedy, Chaos- and Cowboys! The Red Dwarf Companion

Typesetting and layout by PKJ Passion Global

Published in the USA by
BearManor Media
1317 Edgewater Dr #110
Orlando FL 32804
www.BearManorMedia.com

Softcover Edition
ISBN-10:
ISBN-13: 979-8-88771-556-8

Published in the USA by Bear Manor Media

Introduction

One of my all-time favorite films is Almost Famous, Cameron Crowe's 2000 semi-autobiographical comedy-drama about young journalist William Miller (Patrick Fugit), who ends up on tour with a mid-level rock band for a possible Rolling Stone cover feature. For teenaged William, the assignment is a revelation, as he worries about maintaining his objectivity as a writer while growing uncomfortably close to the various members of the band, as well as getting enmeshed in a world of sex, drugs and rock and roll. His best advice comes from a jaded music journalist, who tells him to be honest and 'unmerciful.'

Perhaps not surprisingly, the days of an entertainment journalist spending long stretches of unsupervised time on a shoot are growing increasingly rare. In an era where NDAs and confidentiality agreements have become the norm, producers and studio executives find it ever more important to control their message right down to the last detail. If you don't believe me, just look at how many so-called 'making-of' books are now written by the unit publicist-hardly a bastion of objectivity.

Although I've been on countless film shoots over the course of my three-and-a-half-decade career, I've only been granted two instances of long-term, largely unsupervised access to a project. The first was on Red Dwarf season six in 1993, which I will be talking about here; the other was a British TV series called Neverwhere based on the work of writer Neil Gaiman three years later (my book on the latter will hopefully be published by Bear Manor in the coming months).

With Red Dwarf, I wasn't quite as young as William Miller, but I had only been a full-time freelancer for about a year when I pitched the show's producers on the idea of doing a 'making-of' book. I had previously interviewed them, as well as the entire principal cast for a series of articles in Starlog, which (hopefully) introduced the show to an even bigger US audience, but more importantly, it established my bona fides to the Red Dwarf production office. Even so, I was a bit surprised to be standing in Shepperton Studios notebook in hand, just a few weeks later.

While I can't say my experience matched that of the fictional Almost Famous tour (less drug use, but a lot more bad coffee), there were plenty of similarities. As a journalist, and (gasp!) an American one at that, I was viewed as an object of mistrust for the first week or two. I was referred to as 'the enemy' more than once, and there were a number of occasions when I caught one of the show's stars quietly sneaking peeks over my shoulder to see what I was writing. And plenty of conversations ranging from 'I can't talk while he's here!' to, 'That's okay, he's one of us!'

As it turned out, a good deal of this material would never see the light of day, for reasons I'll explain closer to the end of this book. It's always bugged me a little bit that so much of this story remained untold, so I recently dug out my original notebook, as well as the interviews at the time. For better or worse, I hope I was honest and unmerciful.

Joe Nazzaro
Somewhere in the wilds of New Jersey

Red Dwarf VI Diary

Wednesday, February 10,1993

10:30 AM. Standing just outside the darkened entrance to London's Bankside Power Station, I'm starting to have second thoughts. Following the cast and crew of Red Dwarf for a good chunk of the next two months is going to mean a lot of very long, very cold filming days. Anyone who's ever thought that visiting a film set was a glamorous job would lose those notions the first time an Arctic wind whistled merrily through their nether regions!

It seems highly ironic therefore, that I have no one but myself to blame for this masochistic state of affairs. In December of 1992, I sent a fax to writer/producers Rob Grant and Doug Naylor, pointing out the obvious merits of doing a 'Making of' Red Dwarf book, and adding that I was the obvious choice to write it.

Five weeks later, I'm sitting in the offices of Grant Naylor Productions. Rob and Doug's assistant Helen Norman hands me the first three scripts, 'Psirens,' 'Call Me Legion' and 'Gunmen of the Apocalypse.' She also gives me a brand-spanking-new Red Dwarf crew jacket, which will cause me a few problems during the first day of filming, but I'll get to that in a moment.

Finally, Helen passes me the call sheets for the first block of location filming, which starts in two days. These pages list which cast members will be working each day, what time they have to be on set for makeup and costume, and a breakdown of which scenes will be filmed throughout the day.

The night before filming begins, I finish reading the 'Psirens' script for the umpteenth time, cross-checking scenes against the call sheet to see what will be recorded tomorrow. It's a very funny script, with an opening scene that will definitely surprise a lot of viewers when it airs.

'Psirens' features a very impressive list of guest stars, including former Eastenders star Anita Dobson, Jenny Agutter, who I always remember from such films as Logan's Run and American Werewolf In London, and returning to Red Dwarf after a four-season absence: Clare (C.P.) Grogan as Kochanski. These guest stars only have one small scene apiece, but I'm looking forward to meeting them.

Meanwhile, Sheelagh my fiancée, who's been in the business for more than two decades, tells me to stop thinking about guest stars and concentrate on more practical matters. She runs through a list of things I should remember, including A) When to leave certain crew members alone, B) how to avoid tripping over cables, and C) wearing plenty of warm clothing on location to avoid freezing to death. Hypothermia does not make a good first impression.

Back to the power station. As I enter the building for the first time, I follow option (C). Even with four thick layers of insulation, including a pair of Sheelagh's fluorescent green filming socks, the cold still cuts through me like a ginsu knife (they cut through anything, remember?) Most of the station is inactive, and long lines of orange day-glo tape have been stretched around some of the more precarious areas. This keeps unwary Americans like myself from falling to a messy death, which John the security guard good-naturedly tells me "can be a bit of a nuisance."

10:45 AM. I'm introduced to Bridget Chick the assistant director, a perpetually cheerful girl who leads me to where the first scenes are being shot, one level below where we're standing. "You'll be able to see everything from here!" she chirrups happily, a set of rusty metal steps leading to the lower level. I make myself as comfortable as one can get when perched on an ice-cold metal staircase covered with an inch of rust. By leaning over the safety railing, I can look down into the entire set without breaking, bumping into, or dislodging anything of importance.

I quickly discover that my brand new Red Dwarf crew jacket is going to cause me a few problems. Apparently the crew hasn't been given any jackets, which means that I stick out like a sore, very chilly thumb. Two grips walk by, and seeing my choice of Red Dwarf outerwear, make a few sarcastic remarks about the "privileged few." It's a refrain I'll hear countless times over the next few days, until I learn to say it's much easier to give me a jacket than paying me! That gets a few sympathetic laughs, and the problem is solved.

DATE: WEDNESDAY 10TH FEBRUARY

LOCATION: BANKSIDE POWER STATION
SUMNER STREET SE1
CONTACT - JOHN FARLEY (SECURITY)
TEL: 071 620 8148

DIRECTIONS: SEE MAPS 1 AND 2

SCENES TO SHOOT: EP1 SCENES 3,47PT1,EP2 SCENES 30,32,
EP1 SC47PT2,EP1 SC19
(BUT BE PREPARED TO PICK UP POSSIBLE SCENES FROM THURSDAY'S SCHEDULE)

DAILY SCHEDULE:

UNIT CALL/BREAKFAST	0800 - 0900
TO SHOOT EP1 SC 3,47PT1	0900 - 1300
LUNCH	1300 - 1400
TO SHOOT EP2 SC30,32,EP1 SC47PT2,EP1 SC19	1400 - 1730
EST DE-RIG AND WRAP	1730 - 1800

PARKING: ALL PRIVATE CARS, PARK IN SECOND CARPARK TO LEFT OF POWER STATION (ENTRANCE ON HOLLAND STREET) CATERING AND DINING BUS PARK IN FIRST CARPARK TO LEFT OF POWER STATION (ENTRANCE ON HOLLAND STREET)
GENNY - PARK JUST INSIDE THE ENTRANCE
- AS DIRECTED ON THE DAY. LIGHTING,CAMERA,SOUND, GRIPS,PROPS,MAKE-UP,WARDROBE,-PARK INSIDE THE ACTUAL POWER STATION

ARTIST	CHARACTER	TRANSPORT	M/UP/COS	ON SET
ROBERT LLEWELLYN	KRYTEN	CAB	0615 M/UP	0900
JENNY AGUTTER	PROF. MAMET	CAB	0815 M/UP	0930
CHRIS BARRIE	RIMMER	CAB	1215 M/UP	1400
CRAIG CHARLES	LISTER	CAB	1215 COS	1400
DANNY JOHN JULES	CAT	CAB	1200 M/UP	1400

ALL ARTISTS CALLS AND TRANSPORT TO BE CONFIRMED BY BRIDGET THE DAY BEFORE SHOOTING

CATERING: 53 APPROX

POLICE: SOUTHWARK POLICE STATION 323 BOROUGH HIGH STREET SE1
CONTACT: CHIEF INSPECTOR OF OPERATIONS TEL: 071 407 4759

HOSPITAL: GUY'S HOSPITAL, ST. THOMAS STREET, SE1
CASUALTY DEPT.-ENTRANCE IN NEWCOMEN ST.

SPECIAL REQUIREMENTS:
VISUAL EFFECTS - WOUNDED PSIREN

11:20 AM. The first shot of Red Dwarf VI is Scene 3 of 'Psirens,' where Kryten empties a dustbin into a waste compactor in Starbug's engine room. Each episode is shot out of sequence, with some scenes being shot on location and others on the Red Dwarf stage at Shepperton Studios. The scenes now being shot for example, will be matched up with the smaller engine room set, creating the illusion of a single, massive chamber. It also makes set designer Mel Bibby appear much more talented than he really is, but right now, Mel is too busy to worry about his enhanced reputation. He and assistant Steve Bradshaw have been trying to get the compactor door to work for almost fifteen minutes, without success. Sometimes it slides open and then stubbornly refuses to close. Sometimes it stays smugly closed, and on one occasion, only slides halfway open, giving Robert Llewellyn a nasty blow to his nether regions when he walks into it.

11:40 AM Scene 47. Kryten encounters a wounded Psiren hiding in the engine room. Director Andy DeEmmony walks Robert through the first part of the scene, in which Kryten follows a trail of fluorescent yellow blood across the darkened engine room. This is Andy's first episode of Red Dwarf, and I can't help thinking how nerve- wracking it must be for him. Joining a long- established cast and crew is difficult enough, but Andy also has Rob and Doug on the set, watching every shot on a nearby monitor. If I was to make a comparison, it's like going on your first big date and having your parents as chaperones.

As Andy and Robert continue rehearsing, Jenny Agutter, who will be playing Kryten's creator Professor Mamet, walks on the set, dressed in a silver costume covered by a thick blue ski jacket wrapped around her shoulders. Jenny has seen her share of genre projects, but I don't think she knows much about Red Dwarf. The shocked look on her face when she sees Robert in his Kryten makeup is priceless.

While Andy asks that John Pomphrey's atmospheric green lighting be taken down a notch so the fluorescent blood on the floor can be seen better, Robert amuses the crew by doing his "Kryten's

Granddad" impression. It's the same bit he did for one of the spare heads in 'DNA,' but now it's accompanied by a hilarious, bandy-legged walk, and language that could never be used during family viewing hours. The crew has seen it many times before, but it still draws lots of laughs.

12:00 PM. With Robert sufficiently rehearsed, it's time to get visual effects assistant Paul McGuiness into his Psiren costume. Paul is no stranger to playing monsters; a few years ago, he wore the Drathro costume for the first installment of Doctor Who's 'Trial of A Time Lord,' and more recently, the slavering Curry Monster in 'DNA.'

The insectoid costume Paul is wearing today reminds me of an armored mosquito on steroids. It consists of a massive carapace, dripping feelers, and black reflective eyes the size of King Kong's Ray-Bans. It takes visual FX designer Peter Wragg and two assistants to get Paul into the cumbersome insect outfit.

WEDNESDAY 10TH FEBRUARY 1993 : POWER HOUSE

Item Ep./ Sc./ Pg.	Description	Cast	Location	Costume/ Make-Up	Visual Effects/Design /Props	Extra Notes	Record Dur.
(1) Ep 1/ 3/ 1	STARBUG ENGINE ROOM Kryten emptying garbage.	Kryten	Bankside Power Station	Kryten's Costume Kryten Mask/Hands	Cuboid Garbage Waste Compactor		
(2) Ep 1/ 47 (Pt. 1)/ 2 5	STARBUG ENGINE ROOM Kryten encounters Professor Mamet.	Kryten Professor Mamet (Jenny Agutter) Wounded Psiren (Paul McGuinness)	Bankside Power Station	As Above Luminous Yellow psiren blood	Psi-Scan Bazookoid Walkie Talkie Waste Compactor		
(3) Ep 2/ 30/ 6 8	STARBUG ENGINE ROOM The crew tries to get starbug started by working on the engine housing	Kryten Rimmer Cat Lister	Bankside Power Station	Kryten's Costume Kryten Mask/Hands	Engine Housing : vibrating / lit up		
(4) Ep 2/ 32/ 9	STARBUG ENGINE ROOM The crew being sucked into space	As above	Bankside Power Station	As above			
(5) Ep 1/ 47 (Pt. 2)/ 10	STARBUG ENGINE ROOM Lister, Cat and Rimmer search for Kryten.	Rimmer Cat Lister	Bankside Power Station	As above	Psi Scan Bazookoid Billowing rubbish	Wind Machine	

Having shot the first part of the scene with Kryten entering the engine room, it's now time for him to encounter the wounded Psiren. Paul crouches down in a corner of the set (a difficult task when one is dressed as a seven-foot insect), and Robert walks into the room. It's a deceptively complex sequence, because of the cramped confines of the engine room set, the shadows from the boom mike which creep in when no one is looking, and the general position of the camera. Making things even more difficult, it's virtually impossible for Paul to see or hear inside his Psiren helmet, and the simplest of instructions have to be shouted to him. After three or four takes, Andy finds one he is happy with, and the crew breaks from lunch.

12:15 PM. After a well-deserved break, everyone returns to the engine room set to finish the Kryten/Psiren/Professor Mamet scene. The remaining cast members begin to arrive, and each of them heads for the wardrobe department to try on their new season six costumes. Chris Barrie looks less than comfortable in Rimmer's latest uniform: a quilted red tunic, tight velvet trousers and high-top boots. Dangling from his belt is a device that looks like an expensive pocket calculator, which I later find out is a Space Corps Directive computer. Apparently Rimmer wasn't satisfied with the holographic Space Corps Rule Book he was given in last year's 'Quarantine,' so this season he'll be quoting (or misquoting) Space Corps Directives after consulting this computer.

Craig Charles seems disappointed to lose the well-worn leather togs he's been wearing for the past three seasons. This time, he's been given a boiler suit (which, he informs everyone, makes it much more difficult to use the toilet), a vest, and the now-familiar Lister hat.

As for the Cat, 200 years in deep space hibernation hasn't diminished his sense of sartorial splendor. In season six, he'll be wearing the same black PVC trousers and boots in every episode, but with different jackets, including the tangerine number he's currently sporting.

IMPORTANT NOTICE
RE: SAFETY AT THE POWER STATION

THE POWER STATION IS VERY LARGE AND DARK
WITH LOTS OF HOLES, STEPS, MACHINERY ETC.
FOR YOUR OWN SAFETY PLEASE KEEP TO THE ROUTES
MARKED OUT AND DO NOT STRAY FROM THEM.
ONLY THESE ROUTES WILL BE LIT.

3:15 PM. Jenny is brought back to the set to rehearse the next part of the scene, where the wounded Psiren, disguised as Professor Mamet, orders Kryten to climb into the compactor. Craig and Chris come downstairs to watch Robert's performance, but Robert isn't having a very easy time of it. Even with his new, more flexible costume, he still has a lot of trouble climbing in and out of the oversize prop. Meanwhile, the compactor door continues its "I'll open when I bloody well please" behavior, and I keep waiting for it to slam shut on Robert's head as he recites his last line. Fortunately, that doesn't happen.

4:00 PM. With everyone's attention focused on the Compactor Door From Hell, Rob and Doug worry that some of the scene's dialogue may have been obscured by background noise. A quick playback of the scene confirms their fears, and Andy orders another take from the beginning. What he hopes to do is use a clean audio track from the new take, and combining it with previous takes to produce a scene everyone is happy with. Robert is relieved to be finished. After climbing in and out of the compactor 15-20 times, his knees have turned into Jell-O.\

Jenny Agutter (Professor Mamet)

How did you end up doing this small guest role in Red Dwarf?

Jenny Agutter: It was simply sent to me as a script, and would I be interested? I thought the script was very funny and extremely good, so I said yes. I knew of the series, but I hadn't actually seen it, but I shall now be glued watching it!

What are your feelings on SF in general?

Agutter: It's not my favorite area in film but my tastes are so eclectic, so it can be. It depends entirely on what sort of film is being made. From an actor's standpoint, they're fun to do. What's very good about this is it's a very good and funny script, but on the whole, most SF is quite hard for the actor because it's all about technical stuff. When I did Logan's Run, I spent most of my time acting to blue cloths.

Does that make it more difficult as an actor?

Agutter: It does make it quite difficult to act to nothing! Classical training does nothing to tell you about acting to nothing. The whole idea of acting is to respond to somebody...I can't imagine how hard Roger Rabbit must have been to do. I also did American Werewolf in London, as well as Child's Play II, and a couple of days work on Darkman, which was quite interesting, and now Professor Mamet.

I'm not saying I wouldn't like to be doing it at all, but as an actor, one always wants to be doing something good, and working with good people. There's some science fiction that I wouldn't want to be remembered for; I can't say that I'm particularly thrilled with what Child's Play II turned into. It was a very good Gothic script in the horror genre which worked very well, but by the time we had got halfway through filming, they made so many cuts in the scenes, it was almost impossible to make it work. That was a shame, but if there's anything there at all to play, it's great.

In terms of films, I'm very happy with American Werewolf in London, which really took the genre out of its genre. On *Logan's Run*, I spent a week in a power station like this, just running up and down the corridors shouting, 'No, Logan!' and being wet down every day. It was also shot very slowly. There were big changes in style of lighting, so the setups were very long.

So how did you like this little job?

Agutter: It was terrific; it was great fun to do, because it's a fun part, and the cast is great, and obviously I enjoyed it a great deal.

...

5:00 PM. If Robert thinks he had problems with today's scenes, he's going to be even unhappier with tomorrow's schedule. In the climax of 'Psirens,' Kryten emerges from the compactor and crushed into a small cube. After reading the script I can't help wondering how they're going to do it. When costume designer Howard Burden emerges from the wardrobe trailer, carrying a large, box-like object, I know the answer. The "Cube Kryten" is actually a cardboard costume, with hands protruding from the sides, and a hole on top for Robert's head to emerge. The surface of the cube will be covered with bits of material from Kryten's costume, as well as bits of wire and machinery. For me, it conjures up a mental image of Robert trundling around like a monster from a 1960's William Hartnell episode of Doctor Who.

Meanwhile, Craig, Chris and Danny are rehearsing the last scene of the day, where the crew searches Starbug for the missing Kryten. It's a fairly simple scene, and after an hour of peering around corners and shouting "Kryten!" the boys finally get it right. Kerry the floor manager calls it a wrap, and everybody heads for home.

Thursday, February 11

10:00 AM. We're back at the Bankside Power Station, where filming on 'Psirens' continues. Today's schedule is quite demanding: plenty of camera setups, visual FX, a bunch of new characters, a cubed Kryten, and a seven-foot insectoid. It's going to be a long day.

THURSDAY 11TH FEBRUARY 1993 : POWER HOUSE

Item Ep/ Sc./ Pg.	Description	Cast	Location	Costume/ Make-Up	Visual Effects/Design /Props	Extra Notes	Record Dur.
(1) Ep 1/ Sc 49/ 12	ENGINE ROOM Kryten falls out of the waste compactor	Kryten	Bankside Power Station	Kryten's Cuboid Outfit	Waste Compactor springs open		
(2) Ep 1/ Sc 50/ 13	ENGINE ROOM Insectoid about to suck Lister's brains out. Kryten hurls himself at Insectoid.	Kryten (as cuboid) Insectoid (Paul McGuinness) Lister Cat	Bankside Power Station	Kryten's Cuboid Outfit	Metal Straw Prop Cubed Kryten Insectoid gets crushed		
(3) Ep 1/ Sc 48/ 14 - 15	ENGINE ROOM Rimmer, Cat and Lister unsuccessfuly search for Kryten.	Rimmer Cat Lister Insectoid (Paul McGunness)	Bankside Power Station		Light Bee Drinks Machine Metal Straw	Locked off shot as Rimmer disappears	
(4) Ep 1/ Sc 27/ 16 - 17	CRASHED SHIP Captain Tau begs for help whilst fighting for her life.	Captain Tau (Anita Dobson)	Bankside Power Station	Blood	Smoke Laser Fire Communicator		

Scene 48. Rimmer's batteries fade, and he turns into light bee. Cat and Lister walk fearlessly up to the Psiren, which they see disguised as a drinks machine. The first shot is being recorded one level below yesterday's filming, where the station's massive turbines will be used to simulate another section of Starbug's engine room. In this scene, Lister, Rimmer and the Cat continue their search for Kryten, who unknown to them has been pulverized in the ship's garbage compactor.

As Andy rehearses the three actors for their entrance down a short flight of steps, Peter Wragg is making other preparations. He and assistant Nick Kool are putting the finishing touches on Rimmer's all-new, 1993 light bee, which features a row of blinking green LEDs around its top. Peter attaches a length of wire (which will be virtually invisible on camera) to the bee, and then stands by, waiting for its cue.

10:30 AM. Time for Rimmer to disappear- in a way. As the three actors descend the steps, Chris tells the others he's going to need a recharge, and then steps out of shot. The camera is locked off, and Peter steps in, carrying the light bee. Standing two steps above the actors, he drops the object into Craig's hand as the camera rolls. "And then there were two," the actor mutters.

Andy orders another drop, but Craig ends up taking the instruction literally. He reaches out to catch the falling light bee- and misses! Peter and the rest of the FX crew let out a collective gasp of horror as the expensive prop clatters to the cement floor, but fortunately the damage isn't extensive. After a third and final take, the director says, "Moving on!" and Nick takes the banged-up bee upstairs for a closer examination.

10:45 AM. Andy orders a close-up on Chris, which will be used for Rimmer's fadeout. The first take is okay, and Danny proudly points to his shoulder, the only part of his body in the shot. This naturally prompts various rude comments from the crew regarding which of Danny's other body parts might have better acting ability.

Meanwhile, Paul McGuiness makes his way down the stairs, half-clad in his Psiren costume. The rest of the FX team follows, each of them carrying a piece of insectoid: arms, carapace, headpiece; they look like a team of exterminators coming back from the job of a lifetime.

10:55 AM. With Rimmer gone, Lister and the Cat continue their search for Kryten. They step in front of a drinks machine, unaware that it's actually an illusion created by the Psiren. While the prop vending machine is being assembled, Craig amuses himself by playing an air guitar blues rift on his bazookoid, accompanied by the voice of Danny John-Jules and his world-famous shoulder.

After shooting Lister and Cat in front of the vending machine, the prop is dismantled, and Paul McGuiness is brought on set and positioned in the space previously occupied by the drinks machine, while Danny breaks into an impromptu tap dance on the plastic flooring squares.

Robert Llewellyn, who doesn't have a scene until this afternoon, visits the set, still dressed in civilian clothes. His broad grin indicates he's clearly enjoying his last few hours of freedom. "Is that Part-time Llewellyn?" Craig announces sarcastically. The two actors trade jibes for a few minutes, until Craig is called back to the set for several takes in front of a crouching insectoid.

12:00 PM. Scene 21. Mad Astro speaking to camera black box recording) warning potential viewers of the presence of an insectoid.

The Mad Astro makes his brief but memorable appearance, in a scene moved from this afternoon. The crew has set up in a claustrophobic steel corridor in the power station's basement; a very dark and very scary-looking chamber, crisscrossed by rusted girders that form giant Xs over our heads.

Richard Ridings, AKA the Mad Astro, enters the set. While his face may be unfamiliar to Red Dwarf fans, his voice is instantly recognizable as the DNA Machine in 'DNA.' Richard is dressed from head to toe in black leather trimmed in silver, and looks like a middle-aged, upscale biker. He's joined by Paul McGuiness minus insect head, and Andy runs the actors through the next scene. Ridings is positioned in front of a clear Plexiglas shield, which will distort his features on camera, and Peter's crew begins filling the chamber with smoke.

Paul crouches down between two of the X-shaped girders, and the cameras roll. The script calls for the Mad Astro to address the ship's monitor, while desperately gulping down a hamburger. While he's speaking, a Psiren creeps up and grabs him, spraying a stream of ketchup across the monitor.

The first take goes well, as does the second. Not only does Richard get through his long speech without a single mistake, but he also manages it with a mouthful of hamburger. On the third try, Paul stands up too quickly and hits one of the girders with a protruding feeler, prompting a roar of laughter from the crew. On the fourth try, Richard's speech is a bit too muddled, and Andy comments, "You've got too much food in there, haven't you?"

Finally, by the seventh take, Astro, Psiren and burger all get it right, and the scene finishes with a tremendous spray of ketchup. The director calls a lunch break- "For anyone who's still hungry!"

Richard Ridings (The Mad Astro)

You had done a previous episode of Red Dwarf?

Richard Ridings: Only as a voice-over. I played a computer that was breaking down, and getting things wrong. It was all done in post-production, so I just came into the studio and did a bit of post-synching.

How did you come back to do this episode?

Ridings: I don't know, I think they just thought I was mad enough to do it. They put the camera on me for the audition, and obviously liked what they saw. It seems like a really nice crew, and everyone seems very happy with what they're doing. The scripts are really whacky and very good.

I was amazed you were able to rattle off that entire speech so quickly.

Richard: It was a bit of a worry actually, because the turnaround time on the scripts is sometimes pretty tight. I didn't get mine until Tuesday and it's now what- Thursday? When you've got to do something that quick, it's a bit of a worry.

It didn't help to have to do the speech while eating!

Ridings: That's right, eating the burger and slapping the ketchup all over your face, and reacting with an insect; a hint of Alien as well, which was lovely.

Are you interested in SF at all?

Ridings: Not in a huge way, but I think my credibility with my nieces and nephews has gone right up, by doing one of these!

...

2:00 PM. Scene 27. Captain Tau is under attack from the Psirens. When she is shot dead, a second woman picks up her communicator. It is Kochanski.

After lunch, the crew starts setting up for the next two sequences, which feature a cameo appearance by Anita Dobson, and the long-awaited return of C.P. Grogan as Kochanski. Both actresses are dressed in matching Alien-esque outfits: khaki trousers and T shirts, black vests and armbands. Dobson is wearing an electronic headset, while Grogan wears a floppy hat similar to Lister's. Dobson is obviously excited to be there, while Grogan, who hasn't seen her Red Dwarf costars in several years, is more than a bit nervous. It doesn't help that her scene follows Dobson's; a tough act to follow.

Dobson appears first as Captain Tau; another illusion seen on the ship's monitor. Coincidentally, a female character with the same name appeared in the American Red Dwarf pilot, but I think the resemblance ends there. Dobson plays a kick-ass, rough-and-tumble Ripley-like character, who's trying to fight off a Psiren invasion but is killed by one of the creatures. It's an exciting scene, with explosive charges going off everywhere. Her death scene gets a round of applause from the crew, especially Rob and Doug. I later hear that they wish they had written a longer scene for Dobson, who only appears in the episode for about 30 seconds.

2:45 PM. It's C.P. Grogan's turn to play Aliens, and Andy walks her through the brief scene. I take the opportunity to speak with Anita, who is standing nearby. She's still so charged with adrenaline that she refuses offers of a warm coat from the crew. I'm getting cold just looking at her standing in front of me in a sleeveless T-shirt. "I feel that my credibility has soared to its highest peak now that I've been asked to do Red Dwarf!" she jokes.

Anita laughs, when I ask her if she's going to ask her agent for SF scripts, after enjoying a taste of it on Red Dwarf. "Well, I certainly wouldn't be adverse to reading it! What's so great about fantasy is that anything can happen. You can meet all sorts of weird and wonderful creatures, and weird and wonderful people. I find that very exciting."

Dobson is called back on the set to lie at Grogan's feet for the final part of the scene, where Lister discovers Kochanski is still alive (another illusion of course, but Lister doesn't know that). Craig stands off-camera feeding her lines, and Andy calls for action.

The scene doesn't go smoothly. Grogan blows her lines several times, especially the word "stasis," which she rhymes with Mathis.

With each retake, Peter Wragg's gang has to reset the explosive charges on the set, which is a very annoying and time-consuming process. After six takes, Andy thinks he has enough footage to cut the scene together, and the crew moves on.

4:00 PM. The first photo call of the new season. The four cast members in full makeup and costume are joined by Grogan and Dobson on the star drive set (keep reading) for a round of photographs with longtime stills photographer Mike Vaughan. Not all the poses are for family viewing, but they're certainly fun to watch.

Anita Dobson (Captain Tau)

What made you come in to do one line for this episode?

Anita Dobson: I feel that my credibility has soared to its highest peak now that I've been asked to do Red Dwarf, because it's such a big cult thing for the kids. Everybody watches it and talks about it, so I was happy to come and die for it! I wish I had more to do, because once you've actually come in and become steeped in the whole feel of the thing and put the clothes on, and meet all the guys, I just found myself wanting to do more and more.

What was the most fun part of doing today's scene?

Dobson: I'm an avid fan of sci-fi, so it's been a dream of mine to do one of those glossy movies where you wear all the gear and have all these weird things happening to you. For me, this was realizing a bit of that dream: having a gun, getting dressed up, sweaty and fighting off aliens, things exploding all around me; I loved it!

C.P. Grogan (Kochanski)

How did you end up coming back for this episode, after so many years away?

Clare Grogan: Well, I think you'd have to ask Rob and Doug why the moment was now. As I see it, the thing about Kochanski is she's a tease, and if you get too much of the tease, it loses its effect. Certainly a three-year absence is a bit too much of a tease, and I have no idea why the moment was right in this particular point, but I'm just happy to be back.

Had you said you were willing to come back?

Grogan: I probably hadn't, but I assumed they knew, because we had such good fun in the first couple of series. I was a bit disappointed that we didn't have more of a chance to develop the character back then, because I think there was certainly room for it. But I do think it's her unavailability that makes the whole Kochanski thing funny.

How did it feel to come back today?

Grogan: Very strange. I was very nervous; I know it sounds silly, but there's just a whole feel to the program that it takes you a bit of time to get back into that feeling again, of being here and being part of it, and stepping in from the cold as such; it's very difficult to do.

Even for the one scene?

Grogan: That's actually what makes it harder, in a way, because you've just got this short bit to do, so you've got to make it work and happen right away.

Would you have been happier with an entire story?

Grogan: Yeah probably. Obviously the way this episode happens, we can't do that, but it would still have been really good.

How do you feel about those old episodes now?

Grogan: What made it stranger is no one had any idea that it was going to take off the way it did, so there were no expectations. It was just a new series and everyone on it wanted it to do well.

Is it weird, coming back after your character had been killed off?

Grogan: I just think anything could happen, and that's the beauty of it. People might appear dead or are dead, but there's plenty of room for bringing them back in one way or another. It just means that nobody is ever truly completely dead!

…

With the publicity department satisfied, the crew moves in and starts setting up for their first scene from the second episode, 'Call Me

Legion.' It's the climactic moment, where the crew's newly-installed star drive rips loose from its moorings and punches a hole through Starbug's hull. The resulting decompression leaves the boys literally holding on for dear life.

4:45 PM 'Call Me Legion' Scene 32. Lister, Rimmer, Cat and Kryten are hanging on horizontally for dear life as the vacuum of space tries to suck them out.

The crew of Starbug practices getting sucked into space; one of those events that acting school doesn't really prepare you for. In order to simulate the winds of decompression, a heavy fan is trundled in, and the actors stand on a stack of storage crates, holding onto the bottom of a gantry, with their arms outstretched. By shooting the scene sideways, it will appear as if they are clinging to the railing to avoid being sucked out. Robert has trouble clinging to the gantry with his heavy Kryten gloves, so Andy suggests he cling to Craig's waist. This prompts no end of suggestive remarks from the crew.

The first few takes look a bit silly (or "naff," as the crew says over here), and Andy comments, "You're not desperate enough- you're being sucked out! Try and show as much strain as possible!" The crates are pulled away again, and within a few seconds, the strain on the actors' faces is genuine. By the time Andy gets a take he's happy with, their arms are two inches longer.

5:30 PM. 'Psirens' Scene 48. While Lister and the Cat are attacked by the Psiren (a continuation of the vending machine scene), Robert returns to makeup and costume where he's squeezed into his cuboid outfit In order to simulate the right size and shape, he'll have to shoot his remaining scenes from a crouched position. So much for having an easy day.

While Craig and Danny get the crap beat out of them by a seven-foot bug, and Robert gets ready to do the Red Dwarf shuffle, I take my leave of the Bankside Power Station. It's been a cold two days, and Saturday's not going to be any warmer. That's the trouble with shooting in outer space.

Paul McGuiness (Visual FX)

You started work on season six by building the Psiren?

Paul McGuinness: Mike Tucker made the head and carapace, and I did the underbody and arms. I had already started working on something else when Mike started working on it. We were running out of time, so he did the head while I came on and started doing the underbody and the arms. When Mike finished the head, he started working on the carapace, and Rocky did a bit of carapace as well.

Was it assumed that you were going to be performing it?

McGuinness: Mike was going to do it originally and actually started making an underbody for himself, but Andy came in and saw the plaster cast of my body in the workshop, and said 'Who's that? I like the look of that, because he's quite tall!'

How difficult was it to do?

McGuinness: Doing things like that isn't a problem, because there's not a lot of dialogue. All you've got to do is lumber about in the place where the director wants you to lumber about, and get into the positions he wants you in, so you don't really have to learn anything. Once you get there, there, the director tells you exactly what he wants you to do and it's usually in short bursts; you don't have long periods of stuff that you have to remember, so it's fairly easy.

How can you see out of that mask?

McGuinness: You can't see very much at all. You can't actually tell where you're going or who's in front of you; all you can see is people's feet. Again, that's not a problem, because I didn't have to do a lot of running about. Also the carapace has these big protrusions sticking out, so you have no concept of how big you are either. I was wearing six-inch platforms as well, so I was about seven feet tall. Because you can only see your feet, you don't realize that you've got all this sticking up behind you, so there's a lot of "Duck!" and "Stop!" from the back.

How tough was the quarry night?

McGuinness: I played two different Psirens that night. For the scenes with Craig, Kryten comes in and stabs it in the back with a spear when it's Pete Tranter's sister, and I had to fall over. It was quite rocky ground, and we didn't have any crash mats or anything to fall onto, so I got a few lumps and bumps. The suit has a lot of padding, because it's foam rubber, so I thought it would provide some protection, but the funny thing was, I didn't feel it at the time because it was so cold, and I had to fall over six or seven times, and every time I did it, I put a bump on top of the last bump. I was bit tired and lumpy and stiff after that.

Mike Tucker (Visual FX)

You were involved with the Insectoid for 'Psirens?'

Mike Tucker: At the time the first script turned up, I was the only one on the series, so Peter Wragg asked me to put down some sketches for the insectoid. We sketched out half a dozen ideas for heads and bodies, and faxed them over to Andy, and got a fax back saying, "We like this one!" with arrows all over it, and, 'We like this head because it looks like it's wearing really dark glasses,'

Pete said, 'Right, it's going to be a big build, you'd better get on with it!' so we sculpted up the head and started doing the shell. By the time I got that far, Nick had joined and was getting the bazookoids ready; and then Paul and Rocky joined, so Rocky made up the faceted carapace along the back, while Paul sculpted the body and arms. While that was going on, I was casting pieces in foam and painting them. We basically got the thing assembled just in time for the first OB filming.

While that was going on, I was also making props for the OB, including the small psi scanner, or the 'insectoid detector' as they started calling it.

For Kochanski's gun, they wanted something with cocking action, and I had some props left over from an old Doctor Who episode called 'Earthshock.' They were guns with nice stocks and handles that Martin Bower had made up, so we butchered those. Every year, you know guns are going to come up, and you'll have to build some sort of weapon, so it helps if you've got a stock of basic handguns in stock you can use.

...

Saturday, February 13 Marco Polo Building.

2:00 PM. On the fourth day of OB [outside broadcast] filming, the crew starts work on several scenes from 'Call Me Legion.' The filming takes place in The Marco Polo Building, a high-tech office structure probably best known as the former home of satellite station BSB. Now, many of the offices are disused, making it the perfect place to shoot.

[By the way, I wasn't making a mistake when I said this was the fourth day of filming. Last night, a small crew accompanied Craig, Robert, Paul McGuiness and actress Samantha Robson to a gravel pit in Kent, where they shot the sequence with Lister, Kryten and Pete Tranter's sister (another Psiren in disguise) Because the scenes were being shot at night in a slightly dangerous area, only necessary crew members were permitted. It was strongly suggested to me by producer Justin Judd that it was better not to attend this night of shooting, which was fine with me. The prospect of a twelve-hour night shoot for a single scene wasn't too appealing, especially in the middle of winter].

DATE:	FRIDAY 12TH FEBRUARY
LOCATION:	UNIT BASE:RUGBY CEMENT HALLING, NR. ROCHESTER,KENT CONTACT - MR JOE PEMBERTON 0634 240 261
DIRECTIONS:	SEE MAP 3 AND DIRECTIONS ATTACHED THERE IS A COACH PROVIDED AS CREW TRANSPORT FROM SHEPPERTON
SCENES TO SHOOT:	EP1 SCENE 38

DAILY SCHEDULE:

COACH TO LEAVE SHEPPERTON STUDIOS 'G' STAGE	1445 - 1600
UNIT CALL AND AFTERNOON TEA	1600 - 1700
SHOOT EP1 SC38	1700 - 1900
SUPPER	1900 - 2000
SHOOT EP1 SC38 CONTINUE	2000 - 2300
DE RIG AND WRAP (SNACK ON WRAP)	2300 - 2330

PARKING: IN THE ADMINISTRATION CAR PARK NOT IN THE QUARRY. DO NOT WANDER INTO THE QUARRY UNLESS AUTHORISED

ARTIST	CHARACTER	TRANSPORT	M/UP/COS	ON SET
CRAIG CHARLES	LISTER			1700
ROBERT LLEWELLYN	KRYTEN			2000
SAMANTHA ROBSON	P.TRANTER'S SIS			1700

ALL ARTISTS CALLS AND TRANSPORT TO BE CONFIRMED BY BRIDGET THE DAY BEFORE SHOOTING

CATERING: 51 APPROX

POLICE: CAZENEUVE STREET, ROCHESTER, KENT. TEL: 0634 827055

HOSPITAL: MEDWAY HOSPITAL, WINDMILL ROAD, GILLINGHAM, KENT. TEL: 0634 830000

SPECIAL REQUIREMENTS:
VISUAL EFFECTS: PSIREN
360 DEGREE TURNTABLE

IMPORTANT: A SUREFIRE WELLIE LOCATION

Getting back to today's filming, the area now being used is the Atrium, a gleaming steel and glass three-level enclosure that certainly looks futuristic enough. What's happening is that a tractor beam pulls Starbug into a deserted space station. The crew sets out to explore the station, where they're greeted by the mysterious being known as Legion [played by Nigel Williams].

The first shot calls for our boys to walk to the top of a short staircase and then look around. They're supposed to freeze in place so special FX footage of the will-o-the- wisp entity can be added during post-production.

Unfortunately, the simple scene proves difficult to shoot. What no one realized was that the Marco Polo Building was actually located next to an underground tube line, which means that a loud train passes by every few minutes. For the rest of the day, the now-familiar rumbling noise produces annoyed sighs from cast and crew.

DATE: SATURDAY 13TH FEBRUARY

LOCATION: MARCO POLO BUILDING
CHELSEA BRIDGE, QUEENSTOWN ROAD, LONDON SW8.
CONTACT: HEAD OFFICE, KEN CROUCH 071 782 3181
ONSITE: 071 978 2222

DIRECTIONS: SEE MAP 4

SCENES TO SHOOT: EP2 SCENES 19 AND 20

DAILY SCHEDULE:

UNIT CALL AT UNIT BASE /BRUNCH	1300 - 1400
SHOOT EP2 SC19	1400 - 1830
SUPPER	1830 - 1930
SHOOT EP2 SC20	1930 - 2200
DE RIG AND WRAP (SNACK ON WRAP)	2200 - 2230

PARKING: IN THE MARCO POLO BUILDING CAR PARK
THERE WILL BE UNIT SIGNS

ARTIST	CHARACTER	TRANSPORT	M/UP/COS	ON SET
CRAIG CHARLES	LISTER			1400
ROBERT LLEWELLYN	KRYTEN			1400
CHRIS BARRIE	RIMMER			1400
DANNY JOHN JULES	CAT			1400
LEGION	NIGEL WILLIAMS			1400

ALL ARTISTS CALLS AND TRANSPORT TO BE CONFIRMED BY BRIDGET THE DAY BEFORE SHOOTING

CATERING: 53 APPROX

POLICE: BATTERSEA POLICE, 112 BATTERSEA BRIDGE ROAD, SW11
TEL: 071 350 1122

HOSPITAL: ST.THOMAS HOSPITAL, LAMBETH PALACE ROAD, LONDON SE1 7EH
TEL: 071 928 9292

2:45 PM. Nigel Williams makes his first appearance as Legion. The crew moves to the Atrium's upper level where they shoot the footage needed for the character's materialization. Nigel's shadow is filmed against a white background, first in a crouch, then in a standing position.

Nigel's costume is a metallic green body suit, with a hood that covers most of his head. There's an elaborate molded plastic chest plate in front, with tubes running around the sides, over the shoulders and into a silver mask that covers the actor's face. It's an interesting costume, but perhaps not up the standards of characters such as The Inquisitor. It also makes Williams look a bit potbellied.

While the crew spends the better part of an hour shooting Legion's shadow, I wander downstairs to see what else is happening. Near the entrance, Alan Marshall, one of the visual FX assistants is hard at work on a prosthetic stomach for the scene in which Legion lasers open Lister's stomach, reaches in and pulls out his infected appendix. The false stomach is made of a special material that re-seals itself after being sliced open, and has been cast using Mike Tucker's belly.

Right now, Alan (or Rocky, as I'm quickly informed is his nickname) is busily pasting hair on the false stomach with spirit gum, in order to match Craig's own body. A few minutes later, DeEmmony and Wragg enter the foyer to view Rocky's handiwork and discuss how to shoot it. At some point, I seem to remember that Lister had mentioned having his appendix removed in an earlier episode, but I decide to keep my mouth shut. The crew still isn't used to having me on set, and there's no sense in making waves.

Alan ('Rocky') Marshal (Visual FX)

One of your first assignments for season six was the appendix scene in 'Legion?' Alan ('Rocky') Marshall): That was made from gelatin. We didn't have the actor, so I took a cast from Mike Tucker's stomach helped by Paul McGuinness. I made a silicon mold of Mike's stomach into which I poured a gelatin mix that had been colored to look slightly darker than average flesh tones, based on the coloring given to me by the makeup designer. That was strapped to a dummy with a hole in the back, and a slash was made with a real scalpel, and by pushing the belly from behind, the stomach appears to split on its own, so that when the actor moves the laser scalpel across in front of it, with the addition of a video effect laser beam, the flesh seems to be cut by the laser.

Was it supposed to seal back up?

Marshal: It was, but they didn't shoot a scene, so I presume they'd shoot the opening up and reverse it to seal the stomach. Of course they also wanted to see the actor playing Legion get his fingers inside as he was reaching inside the stomach, which he did, and it looked fine. It needed more slime. It didn't need blood, but it did need slime. I made the appendix as well, which was just a blob of gelatin in a condom.

...

3:30 PM. Scene 20. The humanoid reveals himself to the crew: he wears a mask. The crew starts setting up for Legion's first encounter with the crew. It's a complicated sequence, that will run over two minutes on screen, and includes Lister's appendix removal, as well as Legion converting Rimmer's light bee into hard light mode. I hear a crew member mumble about being there all night on this scene.

While Mel Bibby's crew begins pulling down the fake potted plants from downstairs, other hands are busy setting up for the next scene. Among the props they've brought along is a blinking Plexiglas globe, which appears to be from an old episode of Blake's 7. It turns I'm correct, according to the vis-FX crew, although nobody can remember which episode it came from.

Nick Kool (Visual FX)

You were doing some of the stuff with light bee?

Kool: Oh yes, the light bee needed re-doing. The original one was fairly small, but features quite a bit in this series, because it's taken apart in 'Legion,' and all the wiring is pulled out, so I had to make a light bee that could flip open, which they could pull lots of wiring through. I think we made three: we had one that opened up, one which had flashing lights, which they use to float in the air, and a dummy one for dropping, which was also in the ice cube that Kryten freezes into an ice cube. We also made the saucepan with a wobbly lid so we didn't actually have to drop it in water, which was suggested by the wobbling of the lid. We also put a smoke pellet in the saucepan to get it to smoke

. . .

4:00 PM. Andy runs the cast through the first part of the scene, just up to the point where they meet Legion. It only lasts about 15 seconds, but the sequence still requires several takes. "Okay, we'll do one more," Andy finally announces with a touch of annoyance, "but a lot swifter! With that shot finally in the can, Nigel Williams is called in. Andy calls for an audio check to determine how his voice will sound under the mask. Not too well it turns out, which means his lines will probably have to be re-dubbed later on. Two of Howard Burden's wardrobe assistants step in with cans of green spray paint to touch up Legion's costume- by the end of the night, they'll have used up enough cans to paint a small house.

Andy walks up to Nigel and asks him, "Can you see anything through that thing?" "Yes," the answer booms through the mask, "but I have no peripheral vision."

4:30 PM. There's a problem with Legion's hands. Since they'll be seen in close-up, Andy is worried how the green gloves will look on camera. Comparisons with the Jolly Green Giant are made, prompting a hurried conference with Jeff Jeffrey the Technical Manager, Burden's costume department, and makeup designer Andria Pennell.

"I'd rather go with the skin green than baggy gloves," Andy finally decides, and Andria's team moves in to try out various shades of green makeup.

5:30 PM. At last, Legion meets the crew of Red Dwarf- oops, I mean Starbug. Nigel shakes hands with Robert, and then greets Chris, reaching into his tunic and removing the light bee. A bit of post-production magic will make it appear as though Legion has reached into Rimmer's hologramatic body, which dematerializes into the light bee. Chris will eventually reappear in the identical spot.

"Can we get Chris changed as quickly as possible, please?' The costume people disappear with Chris, who returns a few minutes later, dressed in an identical blue costume. One of the dressers explains that the blue costume will indicate when Rimmer is in his 'hard light' mode, while the red uniform means 'normal' mode.

But wait a minute! Didn't they just shoot the losing scene of 'Legion with Rimmer in his red uniform? I keep that question to myself, thinking maybe I don't understand this filming-out-of-sequence business. That same question will have major consequences several weeks down the road…

Back to the scene at hand. Legion begins to tear apart Rimmer's light bee, pulling endless strands of wire from the device. Nick Kool has constructed several different versions of the light bee, including the one with blinking lights we saw yesterday, a second version without a bottom, so the wires can be pulled through it, and a third bee, which is basically a hollow shell.

After shooting Legion removing long strings of wire from the light bee, Andy cuts the scene, and Nick hands Nigel the hollow version. As the cameras roll, Legion pops a small object into it and snaps the bee shut.

The other three actors are asked to move back, and Nigel throws the revamped device into the air. Chris steps back into the shot in his new uniform where video FX will make him rematerialize.

In order to appear out of nowhere, Chris tries to play his lines off-balance, much as somebody who just stubbed his toe. This causes additional problems for Andy, who's still not 100% familiar with the way the effect will eventually look. "I think you put your arm out on that one," he tells Chris. His response: "I do that anyway, because when you materialize, people will think it's crap!"

While most of the cast and crew break for dinner, Andy, Chris and one of the cameramen stay behind to shoot Rimmer's close-ups.

After a few hours of basically standing around waiting, everybody is hungry and slightly impatient.

7:30 PM. The crew returns from dinner refreshed and ready to get back to work. Chris is back in his red uniform, and he rejoins the other cast members to finish "covering" (shooting the scene from other angles that can be cut together) the scene.

Right away, Robert blows his lines twice in a row while shooting his close-ups. The crew roars with laughter, and Danny shouts, "It's your close-up, Bro!" Robert puts on his Kryten's Granddad face, which I now recognize as exasperation.

To make things even more difficult, there suddenly seems to be a massive increase in train traffic nearby. Robert gets through his lines without difficulty, but the roar of the passing train drowns him out. "Once more, without the train!" Andy announces.

The fifth take is blown by another train, the sixth by yet another. When the seventh attempt is drowned out by the now-dreaded rumbling, Andy look up at the sky with a pained, "Why are you doing this to me?" look. "Fucking train!" he mutters.

8:00 PM. Legion removes Lister's appendix. As Andy rehearses the two actors, Rocky brings in the prop organ in question, a convincingly colored lump of latex. Craig studies the would-be appendix for a moment. "Shouldn't this be hot and steaming a bit?" he inquires. Another quick meeting. How does one heat up a rubber appendix? Peter Wragg suggests immersing it in hot water, so it will steam when exposed to the chilly air. Rocky runs off to find a bucket of boiling water- not an easy task in this deserted office building.

While the crew waits impatiently, perhaps wishing their own organs would warm up, Craig spots the monitor, which shows Legion standing in front of the camera. "It's a bit Doctor Who, isn't it?" he says loudly, indicating Nigel's costume. The remark is made jokingly, but it's said within earshot of Howard Burden, who throws a mock punch at Craig. When the designer turns away, he's not smiling. The joke obviously wasn't funny to at least one person on the set.

8:15 PM. Craig opens his shirt at Legion's request; a task that requires more effort than one would think. Because of the new boiler suit, a lot of unzipping and unsnapping has to take place before the shirt can be opened.

After trying different shots of Craig lifting his T-shirt, Andy finds an angle he's happy with, that has Craig's arms lifted to his chest. The actor sucks in his belly for the camera, but the shot takes some time to set up. "I can't hold it in that long!" moans the uncomfortable Charles. Next to him, Nigel mutters a remark from beneath his mask. Most of it is inaudible, but the words "shake and waddle" can clearly be heard. The crew explodes with laughter, while Craig stands with his stomach (and his dignity) exposed for everyone to see.

8:45 PM. Legion opens Lister's stomach and reaches inside. Rocky's false stomach is set up in front of the camera, and Nigel is given a prop laser scalpel to cut with. An actual razor blade is used to create the incision, with the glowing laser to be added during post-production The extensive computer FX this season are being created by a company called SVC Television, who have sent two of their men, Terry and Carl to observe tonight's shooting. Their presence is necessary to make sure they have the raw footage needed to add the FX.

9:45 PM. Each of the four cast members return to shoot their various close-ups. Constructing a scene is a bit like putting together a jigsaw puzzle. A director usually starts with a "master" or establishing shot, and then shoots the individual close-ups and other angles needed to make the scene more interesting.

The rest of the night is taken up by repetitive camera setups and technical problems- not very exciting stuff, and the crew is starting to look bored and impatient. When a wrap is finally called, everyone is glad to be going home. With the first block of location filming completed, the next step is Shepperton Studios

Thursday, February 18. Shepperton Studios Pre-VT: 'Psirens.'

10:00 AM. By the time I arrive at Stage G in Shepperton, the cast and crew have already finished their morning coffee and bacon rolls, and are busy setting up the first shot of the day.

The next six weeks will follow roughly the same schedule, with one episode being filmed each week. Monday through Wednesday are devoted to rehearsals, during which the script is hammered into shape. On Wednesday afternoon, the cast and crew do a "tech run," where they go through every scene in order, with members of the technical crew in attendance.

Thursday is the Pre-VT Day, in which all the complicated scenes are shot in advance (such as today). Because of the various technical requirements, the Pre- VT is usually the longest and most tiring day of the week.

Friday is a rehearsal/edit day. The cast rehearses while a VT editor cuts together the scenes shot yesterday. These will be played to a studio audience the next day for their laughter and applause. On Saturday, more rehearsals and the occasional last-minute prerecorded scene. The audience is allowed in at 7 PM, and remaining scenes are recorded live.

Stage G is one of Shepperton's older sound stages, and it's obviously seen better days. One of the fire doors is still covered by a crumbling, decades-old movie poster. In the corridor outside the stage are a few overstuffed leather couches that send up small clouds of dust whenever someone sits on them.

At the end of the corridor is a set of stairs that leads up to the production offices and dressing rooms. At the base of the stairs; two makeup rooms and an exit door that leads to the wardrobe department outside. On Saturday nights, a curtain is placed across this area to keep the audience from wandering in and talking to cast members, or "borrowing" props that may be lying around.

On Stage G itself, half the space is devoted to the standing sets, which are laid out in a single line. Since this season takes place entirely on Starbug, each set is a different part of the ship. From left to right, we start with the cockpit, the mid-section, galley, sleeping quarters/ops room, and a section of engine room. There's another chunk of engine room directly behind the sets, connected to the mid-section by an airlock.

Across from the standing sets are several rows of audience seating. The stage can only accommodate about 200 people per recording, and I'm told the show gets requests several times that number every year.

Next to the bleachers, opposite the engine room is a large area reserved for that week's "swing" or strike set. That's where the dining hall for 'Call Me Legion' will be constructed in a few days, as well as the saloon for 'Gunmen of the Apocalypse' the following week.

Today's Pre-VT filming includes several complicated sequences, including an extended split screen featuring two Listers, and a guitarist to double for Craig. The guitar double is none other than Phil Manzanera of Roxy Music fame.

The first scene is 41, with Lister entering the airlock after a near-fatal encounter with a pair of Psirens. Craig is dressed in a quilted silver coat and space boots, and is supposed to be shaken up by his brush with death. "Right, can we do one that's more desperate, more foreboding?" asks Andy. Rob and Doug disagree. They think the take looks fine, but Andy wanted to try a few different approaches to the scene. Reluctantly, the director moves on, and asks Craig to sit in the cockpit set so they can test the lighting.

10:40 AM. The rest of the crew assembles in the cockpit for the next shot. Danny bounces in, showing that boundless energy that never seems to disappear, even after 12 hours of freezing-cold location filming. Howard Burden makes a few last-minute adjustments to his costume, using a wet wipe to clean the vinyl trim of Danny's jacket, as well as the buckles on his wrists and boots. One of Andria's makeup assistants walks up with a small box containing Danny's Cat fangs and hands them to the actor. Danny grins and pops them in without effort.

While the crew is getting ready, Andy and one of his cameramen are shooting a POV shot in the rear engine room set. When Starbug sends a scouter into a derelict space craft, it sends back a probe of what it sees. What Andy is now shooting will look like a searchlight beam moving down a darkened corridor.

11:00 AM. Scene 43. Cat starts to take off. Danny sits in cockpit, while Andy offers ways to adjust the controls. "Can we put one hand on the steering column?" he suggests.

11:15 AM. Scene 22. The boys watch the Mad Astro's death on a monitor and Rimmer falls backwards in a dead faint. Robert enters the cockpit, in full Kryten makeup. His dresser Paul trails behind, pouring talcum powder into a pair of Kryten gloves so they can be pulled on easily. Two other assistants make final adjustments to his costume, one of them wielding a large sewing needle. Robert tries to stand quietly, but he's obviously quite nervous about having a long, sharp object near a certain part of his anatomy.

Up close, Robert's Kryten mask is a beautifully designed piece of work, and it's absolutely fascinating to see him transformed by it. Visitors on the set (and there are a lot of them) often ask if they can touch his head, extending one hand forward with the same timidity they would have if they were petting a large snake.

Craig walks onto the stage, followed by Chris carrying a cup of coffee. "Can we have the artists in the cockpit please?" calls Simon Wallace the floor manager. The FX men bring in a pile of mats to be placed behind Chris to break his fall. After rehearsing the scene, Andy calls for a take. With each attempt, he orders small adjustments, first asking Chris to start his faint a beat earlier, then moving Robert a few inches over so his costume doesn't reflect the light. The fourth take he proclaims as excellent.

11:45 AM. Scene 23A. Kryten wandering around engine room . "Kryten in the engine room please!" calls Simon. Unfortunately, Robert is in no condition to move, as most of the costume department swarms around his lower regions with scissors, needle and thread. When Craig walks by accompanied by a small group of female visitors, he waves to his mechanoid costar, who quips, "I'm having my groin attended to!"

Meanwhile, Peter Wragg's FX team is in the cockpit, rehearsing a scene where Starbug is struck by a meteor and the impact throws Rimmer backwards through the cockpit door. The effect will be achieved by a leather harness hidden beneath the actor's costume, and Peter is making sure that everything runs smoothly. As Paul McGuiness stands in as Rimmer, the team runs through the stunt over and over until it's perfect.

With Robert's groin attended to, he's ready for his scene. These shots of Kryten walking through the engine room will be combined with the rest of the sequence shot at the Power Station. Because the studio set is much smaller, Andy tries to shoot Robert in close-up to make it more interesting. "We don't need to go so far away," he instructs the cameraman.

12:05 PM. Scene 34. Rimmer gets flung backwards through the cockpit door. Smoke and sparks fly from consoles. Chris returns to the set, strapped into his stunt man harness. The rest of the cast seat themselves in the cockpit to watch Peter Wragg yank Chris through the door with a thick rope.

12:35 PM. Ready to record. Rimmer explains to the others that they're quite safe, that the meteor headed for the ship is a telepathic illusion. Sudden impact; red lights flare, sparks fly, and Rimmer flies through the air- at least that's what is supposed to happen. Chris blows his line on the first take, and subsequent tries don't look very convincing.

Finally, Rocket the senior cameraman moves into the set with a small, hand-held camera to shoot up at Chris as he's pulled out the door. "That works better for me," he tells Andy on the next take. Danny suggests a slightly different way of choreographing the stunt, which actually looks better. They try one more take, and the shot is in the can.

2:20 PM. Scene 36. Cat and Lister are trying to put out fires. Rimmer staggers in. Kryten explains that part of Starbug is embedded in rock, and Lister volunteers to go outside to sort the problem out.

When it comes to dialogue, Robert Llewellyn is the unsung hero of Red Dwarf. Line for line, he probably has more dialogue than the other three cast members combined. What looks easy on screen, however, is a different story on the studio floor.

Robert's current tongue-twister is the line, "The front landing stanchion is embedded in the rock up to its joint." In take after take, the scene goes smoothly up to that point, but Robert just can't wrap his lips around "landing stanchion." "I don't know the fucking line!" he snaps impatiently, and Craig quips, "He's only had his first joint!" Eventually, Robert gets the line, and moves on.

3:05 PM. "You sort out the engines," says Craig. "I'll be out there being brave, two minutes maximum." As he walks out of the cockpit, Robert gives him an adoring, "What a guy!" look that breaks everybody up. Regrettably, the look is eventually cut from the final version.

3:20 PM. Scene 39. Rimmer and Kryten craning over the mic. While Robert and Chris speak into a mike in the cockpit, Craig reads his lines off-camera. That's followed by Scene 40, where Kryten sees Lister on the monitor and pushes a button to let him in.

3:55 PM. Scene 44. A second Lister appears on the screen as Lister 1 and Kryten head off towards the cockpit. Craig takes exception to the line, "For God's sake, I can't hang on any longer!" Quite rightly, he points out that it's not something Lister would say, and suggests "For Smeg's sake" instead. Since Rob and Doug aren't on the set, Andy decides to go with the line as written.

The scene runs into an unexpected snag when the airlock doors fail to full open, and Craig walks into them. On the next take, they don't open fast enough, and Andy tries several more times to get them to open properly.

5:00 PM. Scene 46. The two Listers are seated side by side. Cat, Rimmer and Kryten try to devise various tests to discover which Lister is real.

The next few hours will be spent shooting the most challenging scene in Psirens: a split screen sequence featuring two identical Listers. Each shot has to be done in four passes: Lister 2/Kryten/Rimmer/Cat, Lister 1/Rimmer, Lister 2/Rimmer and Lister 1/Cat/Kryten. This is Andy's first split screen for Red Dwarf, and he has every shot mapped carefully mapped out in advance.

The first part of the scene to be shot is Lister 1 playing the guitar like a diva. The script describes it as "A superb display of axemanship," and to make the scene convincing, the producers have brought in Roxy Music's Phil Manzanera to do the honors. Originally they had hoped to get Queen's Brian May to do the unseen cameo, but when May had to go on tour, Manzanera, a devoted Red Dwarf fan, was asked to do it instead.

Craig is already seated in his chair when Manzanera walks in, dressed in identical, loose-fitting long johns. He takes the second seat, and while Andy shoots him playing the guitar from the neck down, Craig looks on with a bored expression, as though he's actually watching himself. The guitar solo elicits a round of applause from the crew.

With Manzanera's work done, the musician heads back to wardrobe to change into his street clothes. The crew gets ready to shoot the first pass. Since Craig can't be in both places at the same time, stage manager Rina Konstantinou stands in for the other Lister. "She's Greek," jokes Craig, parodying his line in the script, "She doesn't have my classic profile!

As the scene winds on, Andria Pennell steps in during a break to do some quick repair work on Robert's mask. She picks up a pair of prop scissors that were actually being used in the scene, and when she finishes, mistakenly hands them to the costume department. The loss is discovered a few minutes later, when Kryten goes to pick up the two pairs of scissors- and only finds one pair. "I've lost my scissors," he announces with genuine puzzlement.

5:45 PM. The two Listers describe the tattoo on their left buttock…

The joke takes almost half an hour to shoot, but is ultimately cut from the sequence, which runs on too long. It's also a sequence that Craig isn't too happy with. After a take that looks good to everyone else, he asks Andy if he can do his Ganymedian monk speech again. Subsequent passes look fine, but there is still a bit of dialogue Craig doesn't like. "Are the writers around?" he asks. A quick search of Stage G fails to produce Rob and Doug who have headed back to their office in London. The line stays.

Lost scenes: The two Listers. A longer version of scene #46 was filmed, but a large part of it was cut from the final episode:

RIMMER: A series of questions to trick and confuse you. If you fail to *answer correctly, or for any reason hesitate you'll be shot.*

LISTER 1: Come on Rimmer, give us a break.

LISTER 2: (Overlapping) For God's sake, Rimmer, do me a lemon.

RIMMER: Kryten?

KRYTEN throws two apples. Both LISTERS catch them right-handed.

RIMMER: Both right-handed. Correct. You have a tattoo on your left buttock, true or false?

LISTER 1&2 (Together): true.

RIMMER (To LISTER 1): You. It's dedicated to the one unbending love of your life. Describe the tattoo?

*LISTER 1: It's a heart with an arrow thro*ugh it, and underneath it says, "I love vindaloo" in dripping curry sauce.

RIMMER (To LISTER 2): You. How did you get it?

LISTER 2: Planet leave on Ganymede. Went on the razz with Peterson. He spiked my cocktail with half a pint of four-star petrol. When I *next awoke, I'd enrolled as a novice monk in a Ganymedian monastery. I discovered the vindaloo tattoo when I handed in my habit.*

(The rest of the scene continues as aired)

...

7:10 PM. After breaking for dinner, the crew starts drifting back to the set. While we've been away, Mel Bibby's crew has been hard at work on a small set which will be used for the Temptresses- two voluptuous models who will be seen only on the ship's monitor.

The set looks like it's been set up for a Roman orgy. Every square inch it is decorated with luxurious draperies, wall hangings and pillows, and is lit with a soft purple lamp. In the front, a large sea shell, and a massive, overturned urn, spilling over with grapes and other artificial fruit A few crew members ask (with professional interest of course) when the two Temptresses will be coming in.

Meanwhile, the remaining cast and crew assemble in the mid-section, to finish Scene 46. Chris Barrie returns, in full Rimmer costume. He picks up Lister's guitar and strums a few tinny notes. Craig straggles in, still clad in baggy long johns, and sits cross-legged in one of the chairs.

By 7:30, most of the scene has been shot except for a few pickups. Each movement has to be carefully choreographed so the actors don't walk into the wrong half of a split, which makes the entire process considerably more complicated. With the scene almost finished, Peter Wragg tells Paul McGuiness to put on his Psiren costume.

8:25 PM. The crew starts setting up for the final shots, where Kryten and Cat blast the false Lister with bazookoid fire, revealing him to be a Psiren. While they're getting ready, Craig wanders over to me. "Are you getting bored yet?" he asks, seeing me making notes. He quizzes me on what I think of the new season, his new costume, and do I think this episode is funny. I try to be diplomatic as possible. Over the next few weeks, Craig is the only cast member who's often acutely aware of my presence, and that I'm quietly recording much of what is happening. "Is this going to be in the book, then?" becomes a regular question, sometimes asked good-naturedly, sometimes not. Wragg walks up to Paul McGuiness, who is standing a few feet in front of me, half-clad in Psiren garb. "Paul, put your arms on!" he instructs his assistant.

8:50 PM. Rehearsal finished, the FX team brings their Psiren back to set. Small explosive squibs are wired into the costume to simulate bazookoid hits- Andy asks for six charges. Mike Tucker uses a wet wipe to clean off the Psiren's huge, reflective eyes, and Paul is positioned in the same spot previously occupied by Lister #1.

"I only want to do this once!" Andy tells the crew, and call for action. Sparks fly, as each charge is ignited, and the insectoid falls to the ground. The director plays the scene back on a nearby monitor. "Absolutely perfect," he says. "Thank you."

9:00 PM. The final part of the scene sees Cat and Kryten blasting the bogus Lister, with Rimmer looking on. As the three actors rehearse the scene, Chris flubs a line, and without missing a beat, Robert, still in character, asks, "Are you sure that's the right line, sir?"

While Andy instructs the actors in how to hold their weapons ("hold them up, so I can get a smoking shot as well,") the two temptresses arrive, seating themselves in the upper rows of audience seating. The two girls who play the Temptresses are Liz Anson and Zoe Hilson, and their sexy costumes draw an inordinate amount of attention. Crew members suddenly start finding reasons to stop by; retrieving pens from their jackets that have been left in that area, or studying their scripts with exaggerated care.

9:40 PM. Scene 25. Two beautiful Temptresses appear on the monitor, begging for help as their settlement is almost extinct. They need seed spreaders (don't we all!).

[That last comment is from the camera script by the way, not a personal observation.] The last scene of the day involves the two Temptresses, who are recording a scene that will be played over the ship's monitor. Since the crew is supposed to be finished by 10 PM, there's a sudden flurry of activity as Andy tells them he wants this last scene finished. If the shot isn't in the can today, they'll have to bring both actresses back and pay them for an extra day.

Although the four cast members are not actually involved in the last scene, most of them decide to stay around. Watching the two actresses rehearse various seductive positions on the set, it's not difficult to understand why.

After running the Temptresses through their scene, Andy calls for a take. The first one isn't quite there, and there's only time for a few tries. On the last take, Robert (now clad in a bathrobe) watches the playback on a nearby monitor and proclaims, "I'll buy that for a dollar!" Andy looks less happy with the scene, but there's no time to do it again. He'll just have to settle for the last take, and Simon calls it a wrap.

Saturday, February 20. Audience Recording Day: 'Psirens'

5:00 PM. The first half of the day is taken up with rehearsals for tonight's scenes. The cast, still in civilian clothes, run through each scene with Andy (and usually Rob and Doug looking on).

Today's routine is slightly different from other Saturdays, because an additional scene has to be recorded in advance. The opening scene, of Lister emerging from suspended animation, a la Alien, was supposed to have been recorded on Thursday, but the crew simply ran out of time. That means tonight's schedule is going to be more hectic than usual.

5:15 PM. Robert and Craig are sent to makeup. Normally only Robert has an early makeup call (which means he usually misses dinner), but Craig also has to be prepared for his first scene, which will be recorded within the next hour.

Meanwhile, people begin to filter in. Technically, the set is supposed to be closed to the general public with the exception of the Saturday-night audience, but a lot of people involved with the production usually show up a bit early. I recognize Charles Armitage, one of the directors of Noel Gay Television, who's also Rob and

Doug's agent. We've been communicating with each other by fax for the last few months, but this is the first time we actually meet. He's a big, burly guy, like a retired wrestler.

I also see Rob and Doug's assistant Helen, who waves and quietly stands in the background. She's accompanied by Kate Cotton, the publicist for the series, who I've known for a few years.

Kate starts walking around the sets with Mike Vaughan, *Red Dwarf's* long-time stills photographer. They're talking about taking pictures of the cast and crew reading Red Dwarf Magazine, to use for upcoming interviews (many of which are mine). I suggest grabbing Mel Bibby, who's walking around in his brand new crew jacket, and putting him behind one of his cockpit sets. The three of us drag the reluctant Mel to his first photo opportunity, followed by an equally shy Peter Wragg.

6:00 PM. Scene 2. Lister emerges from deep sleep unit. Craig staggers onto the stage, dressed in long johns, a wig and beard of astonishing length, as well as six-inch finger and toenails. As everyone laughs at the strange sight, Craig walks carefully to the ops room which has been redressed as a hibernation set. He asks Rob and Doug what he should do after awakening, and Doug suggests moving very slowly to allow the audience to react. "You're going to get roars, so don't go straight for it," he tells the actor.

Craig lies down on the bed, and immediately one of his fingernails pops off. It's a sight that will be repeated numerous times over the next few hours. Simon calls for the bed to be raised (Mel's stage hands lifting it by pulley off-camera), but the platform raises too high too fast, and a stifled cry is heard from within the compartment.

The camera pans from a window filled with stars, and over to the bed as it slowly descends, accompanied by clouds of dry ice. The chamber fills with light, as one by one, monitors and light fixtures blink to life.

Several takes are shot, with the bed descending at different speeds. A few feet away, Mel's crew is starting to get red-faced from the effort of lifting Craig into the air over and over again.

With that shot in the can, it's time for the awakening. As Craig slowly rises from his bed, the camera cuts to his feet and back to a full-length shot of Lister as he staggers across the room to a nearby table. Inserting one of his long fingernails into a pencil sharpener, he catches sight of his reflection in a blinking monitor screen and asks, "Who the hell are you?

That's followed by a quick shot of Lister scratching himself, which looks fine, but Andy orders another take. "Let's have the scratch on the sit, not the stand," he orders.

7:00 PM. After an abbreviated dinner break, the crew returns to the stage as the audience begins to arrive. The number of seats has been badly overbooked, but some fans are allowed to stand on the steps at the end of each row. Since the seats are given out on a first-come, first- serve basis, a lot of late-comers find themselves disappointed, but extra seats have been placed in the corridor outside the stage so they can watch the recording on the monitor. It's not too much of a disappointment for them; they get the first glimpse of cast members coming out of makeup, some of whom sometimes stop for a quick word or autograph.

Just before the audience is allowed in, I'm asked if I want to sit in the front or if I'd rather stand in the wings. The prospect of sitting for more than three straight hours in a cramped audience isn't very appealing, and I'd rather stand. It's a better choice, because I can walk back and forth behind the seating to watch what's happening on both sides, and occasionally nip outside to talk with people outside the stage door.

7:25 PM. Andy Bull, the show's warm-up man is introduced. Rather than using a standup comic as many sitcoms do, the producers have decided to use a variety player who can interact directly with the audience. Andy's bag of tricks includes a unicycle, juggling equipment, and a few copies of Red Dwarf Magazine, hastily autographed by the cast as prizes.

7:45 PM. Andy introduces Danny, Chris and Robert to the audience, and Robert stays on stage for the first scene. Craig's appearance has been kept secret to preserve the impact of the first scene. He's standing at the top of the gantry leading into the mid-section, out of sight.

The familiar opening credits are played over the Stage G's speakers, and the audience erupts with deafening applause. The monitors light up with the Red Dwarf logo, and the noise dies down. Each episode is shown to the audience as completely as possible. Although the model shots and other visual FX obviously won't be ready for many months, the OB and Pre-VT scenes have been loosely edited together for the audience's reaction. Those scenes are played over the monitors in-between the live scenes.

As the first, hastily-edited scene of Lister awakening from cold sleep is seen, there's a moment of stunned silence from the audience, followed by laughter as they realize who it is. I look over at Rob and Doug who are standing near a monitor. They're both smiling, and it's easy to see why: the audience is hooked.

7:45 PM. Scene 4. Kryten explains to Lister that he has been in a deep sleep for 200 years. As the first live scene begins, Kryten tries to explain to Lister (and indirectly, the audience) what has happened. When Robert blows his first line, there is a roar of laughter. Craig turns to the audience. "Actually, I haven't been introduced yet," he tells them. "I play Dave Lister." Burst of applause.

Robert is still having trouble getting into the rhythm of the scene. "One day, your mouth is your own," he declares, "and the next, it belongs to someone 300 miles away!" By the fourth take, a slightly exasperated Craig declares, "I don't think I'm ever going to get to the end of this scene!" A few minutes later, Robert tries to inject Craig with a synaptic enhancer, and when he looks down, jokes, "I've just squirted the synaptic enhancer all over my suit." Mercifully, the scene is finally finished, and Craig goes off to get into his costume.

8:10 PM. Scene 6. Kryten brings Rimmer to life via the computer. Although most of the electronic FX can't be completed until post-production, SVC has provided one sequence in time for tonight's recording. When Kryten re-boots Rimmer's light bee using the ship's computer, a CG scene shows the character's personality being downloaded. The sequence will be combined with Robert's voice-over, as well as live action footage of Rimmer materializing, to be shot in front of blue screen.

8:30 PM. Scene 7. Crew eating breakfast, explanation as to what has happened to Red Dwarf.

With all the actors in the mid-section, the recording continues. A few minutes later, Chris blows a line, prompting Robert to tell his co-star, "Don't worry, you're joining a cast of well-trained professionals!" It requires several takes to get their lines correct, but Andy finally decides he has enough to put the scene together.

8:45 PM. Scene 10. All at their stations. Orange light flares from the right. Cat wrenches controls to the left.

The next scene appears to be going well until Danny forgets his next line. He grins guiltily, looking around him for help. None is forthcoming. "Anything else coming, Mr. Cat?" Robert finally asks, in an attempt to feed the line. It goes downhill from there, as Robert starts forgetting his own lines. Danny also has trouble, because he keeps forgetting to sniff. In the new season, Cat's olfactory sense has become sharp enough to sense oncoming danger, but it's difficult to remember your line while sniffing at the same time.

9:10 PM. The crew scans the wreckage of a derelict ship. The scene goes well, leading into the Mad Astro sequence, which is played for the audience. The scene elicits groans of disgust when a stream of ketchup hits the screen, and that creates a technical problem. The audience groans so loudly when they see the ketchup, they obscure the Mad Astro's line, "You've squeezed the ketchup out of my burger!" The line is eventually magnified, but even in the final version, it's still difficult to hear.

9:30 PM. The others confirm Cat's suspicion that the Temptresses are in fact, the Psirens.

What should be a simple scene takes a surprisingly long time to shoot. Most of the dialogue is Danny's, and involves his running from the mid-section to the cockpit, but his usually flawless timing is off. It takes several attempts to finish the scene.

*Lost Scenes: Lister plays Pinball Wizard with meteors. In the first draft of 'Psirens,' scenes 11-19 had Lister destroying a meteor by changing Starbug into a giant pinball machine. In later drafts, the sequence was simplified, using the ship's waste d*isposal system and a souped-up cube of garbage.

...

9:45 PM. While the audience is watching the playback of the two Listers, I slip out into the corridor for a quick cup of coffee. Outside the stage, a small crowd of fans are watching the scene on a monitor. The split screen effect is very convincing, and the sequence gets plenty of laughs.

Robert walks through the stage door and heads for the wardrobe department to remove his costume. He now has to switch into the cube Kryten outfit for the final scene. While he's waiting for the costume to be prepared, he comes up behind me to watch the monitor. The sight of Robert in his Kryten mask, wearing sweats and sneakers is a strange one indeed. It's as though he's getting ready to shoot a Red Dwarf exercise video.

10:15 PM. Scene 52. Life returns to normal for the time being. Robert, now dressed in his cube Kryten costume, takes his place in the cockpit. The recording should have ended 15 minutes ago, so there's some tension in the air about filming this last scene as quickly as possible. Fortunately, there's no real problem. When the last take is finished, Robert springs to his feet, and Craig starts chanting the Red Dwarf theme song. The audience applauds and cheers loudly, and then everybody heads to the studio pub for a drink. The first episode of Red Dwarf VI is in the can.

Thursday, February 25. Pre-VT Day: 'Call Me Legion'

10:00 AM. As I walk onto Stage G, 1 grab a copy of today's camera script from a box placed near the front row of audience seating. A few crew members are standing around, looking at their own copies and shaking their head. Glancing through the schedule, I can see why. While the number of shots scheduled for today is relatively small, most of them are extremely complex. Scenes #21 and 21A, which take place in Legion's dining hall, appear to be the most difficult. Lots of floating food, Mimosean anti-matter chopsticks and other time- consuming FX that will eat up the day's schedule very quickly.

The four cast members are already in costume and makeup, and are already rehearsing the first scene. Since Nigel Williams is still getting into his Legion costume, Rina the stage manager is standing for the actor.

On the far side of the stage. Legion's elaborate dining hall set has been constructed. Mel Bibby has taken some of the high-tech elements from the Marco Polo Building and added a number of his own interesting touches. The walls are covered with metal shelving, large paintings and murals, while bits of art and statuary dot the room. The floor has been covered with gleaming black and white tiling, and in the center, a modern dining table and several high-backed chairs.

Off-stage, another table is covered with strange- looking props that will be used in the dining hall scenes. There is one tray of edible food, another inedible. A plate of hairy objects that look like small Tribbles has been prepared, and a few feet away, looking terribly lonely, is the never-seen Despair Squid that was built for last season's story, 'Back to Reality.' Peter Wragg's assistant Rocky is putting the finishing touches on one of the dishes; cutting long lengths of black cord which he uses to garnish the meal. Each dish is then placed on a trolley, which Legion will wheel into the dining room.

Rocky uncovers a small bucket of dark blue liquid and prepares to pour it over the "edible food" dish. "Is this the edible blue?" he asks no one in particular. With that confirmed, he pours out a generous helping of the azure liquid. Retrieving a bucket of green liquid, he repeats the process on another dish.

Meanwhile, Mel and his crew are tinkering with the star drive prop, which is sitting in one of the unused sets. The star drive has actually been constructed by Vendetta FX, who are also located in Shepperton, and run by former Blake's 7 FX man, Jim Francis. Because there's so little time to build the specialized props needed for Red Dwarf, Mel will sometimes farm them out to Vendetta, who work very quickly. As the device is switched on, lights begin to blink, and the top part spins rapidly. So far, so good.

10:15 AM. Scene 21. While Legion departs the room to prepare their food, the crew discusses his position and decide to invite him to join them. Legion enters with a food-laden trolley: a traditional, 24th century Mimosean banquet.

Nigel Williams arrives on the set, dressed in his now-familiar green costume. Simon the floor manager checks his watch and realizes they're running behind. He orders the exterior doors to the set rolled shut (this is where Legion will make his entrance) and wonders, "Have we trapped anyone out there? As long as it's not the cast members, that's all right."

Nick Kool steps onto the set with a large glass container filled with green liquid. One by one, he fills each of the glasses on the table. John Pomphrey, the show's veteran lighting director, studies the color of the room, trying to decide if he should use a red lighting gel or a peacock blue one. He decides to go with the latter. "It breaks up the blue-ness of the room," he explains to me.

As Rocky and Nick finish putting together the latest in Mimosean cuisine, I look at some of the strange items they've assembled. One in particular looks strangely familiar; a long, foam rubber tentacle covered with large suckers. Nick tells me it's actually a Despair Squid tentacle that was built for an underwater model shot. Like the squid itself, the tentacle was also cut from the final version of 'Back to Reality,' and Rocky is hoping that some of his handiwork may ultimately be seen in this episode.

Nick Kool (Visual FX)

Kool: With the Mimosian chop sticks. They were described as tremendously complicated-looking TV aerials, and I knew I had to make ten of them, so they had to be made fairly easily to look the same, I bent aluminum rods into an interesting shape, and dressed them with Perspex, because Peter wanted to have them illuminated which in the end we really didn't have time to do, but the perspex we used was fairly luminous, so we had to hope the studio lights would catch them the right way.

We also had a problem with the motors. They were supposed to revolve, so I had little nylon gear boxes which made quite a bit of noise. We could have used better motors, but to make ten of them would have been too expensive. They also had to fit in the handle, so I spent about a week making these ten chopsticks. What I wanted was something that would look like an actual eating implement, not like a weapon. They also had to look fairly delicate since they would be eating at a table with them, but at the same time, the actors were making strange movements with them, trying to elevate their food, and so on. I think originally, they were going to try and wind food up in them as well, and eat off them, but that proved to be too difficult, so in the end, the food never actually touches them. I was quite relieved that nothing broke, because if one of them did go down, I had ten of them we could chop and change, but there were shots where we all had them going at the same time.

That brings us to the space station for 'Legion.'

Kool: I made a few thumbnail sketches of what I thought was quite an elegant shape. I was thinking of the Marco Polo Building which was very clean and brightly lit, so I went with an almost art deco look, with lots of rings. We wanted to do something different, because we had done a space station for 'Justice,' so we were trying to get away from the usual space station shape. Mike wanted to do a hanger with a lot of curves, and I had the idea of doing circular sections, so he started building his section of the hanger, and I kept it in mind when I started building the model, so hopefully it should tie together quite nicely.

Usually the shots are only a few seconds, because there's only so much the viewer can take in of the actual structure, but I still put in the finer detail that you usually don't get to see; it gives it scale, even though it doesn't have time to register on screen. Sometimes you do a model, and they decide they want to do a really tight shot on it, and you find yourself sticking a bit more detail on it in certain places, so you have to try and guess how close you're going to get.

Mike Tucker (Visual FX)

Tucker: The station itself is being built by Nick, so he came up with a basic design, which is being adapted slightly now that we've seen the location. The station has a swooping, almost bat symbol feel, which I've echoed in the landing pad. The rest of the station is very much based on the Marco Polo Building where we were filming, so the tiled floor was literally done at the last minute when I saw Mel's set.

…

10:50 AM. Prepare to start recording. Despite Nigel William's limited vision, the scene goes very well. Legion enters the dining hall from a false corridor, pushing the serving trolley in front of him. Kryten picks up a cloth napkin and like a well-trained waiter, drapes it over his arm.

12:00 PM. Scene 26. Cast faces in blue neck braces for morph sequence. The climactic sequence of the episode takes place when Lister accidentally dislodges Legion's mask, revealing the entity's face to be an amalgam of Lister, Rimmer, Cat and Kryten. Although the effect will be created electronically by SVC, it will require live-action footage of the four characters. To that end, each actor has to be filmed in front of a blue screen, using a neck brace to keep their heads in synch.

The first to be shot is the Cat, and Danny walks in, wearing a simpler version of Legion's costume. Upon seeing him, Nigel jumps from his seat, and the two actors link arms and dance around the stage.

Finally, Danny is stood in front of the blue screen and clamped into place. Nigel stands off-camera, so his line, "Now look what you made me do!" can be recorded at the same time.

For several minutes, Andy coaches Danny in a variety of facial expressions- "Show me the teeth...yeah, that's quite nice...now show me the teeth a bit more..." After a number of expressions have been shot, Nigel recites his line while Danny moves his lips to the words. After several run-throughs, Danny spreads his arms in triumph. "The King of Mime!" he announces to the crew's applause. "I'm not surprised, I spend all summer doing it on Maid Marion!"

12:05 PM. Danny is removed, and Robert is stood in front of the screen. A still frame from the previous footage is played back, so Andy can compare the two heads. There's an obvious problem, because Robert's head as Kryten is considerably larger than Danny's and difficult to line up. Finally, Andy is ready to record, and Nigel recites his line to be spoken by Kryten

12:15 PM. "Is Chris here?" asks Andy. Barrie gets up from his seat and is clamped in position. "Don't worry about the suit, folks; it's the head we're looking at!" the director announces, and in a moment we see why. On the monitor, Rimmer's costume disappears against the blue screen, leaving what amounts to a disembodied head.

After checking the shot, Andy asks for a hair band to pull back Chris's hair, and Andria Pennell runs off to find one.

While they're waiting, Craig is put in the clamp. Unlike his three co-stars, he's obviously ill at ease standing in one place, and begins to fidget. "Craig, stay absolutely still, please!" says Andy, with obvious annoyance. "Rigid as possible there...can we record please?" Nigel runs his lines over Lister's angry expression, and an obviously relieved Craig is dismissed.

12:25 PM. Chris minces in, wearing a very feminine-looking hair band. The crew reacts in obvious fashion, but Chris takes it in stride. “Sorry, I did ask for a manly one,” says Andy, referring to his actor’s new head gear. Chris turns serious as soon as he steps in front of the camera, and his scene is shot without incident. “Lovely, thanks very much,” the director announces.

Before the crew breaks for lunch, there’s still a few more blue screen shots to finish. For a scene in which Rimmer reaches inside his own body to extract his light bee, Chris is placed in front of the blue screen, holding a piece of white poly board before him. As the camera rolls, he “reaches into it.”

Meanwhile, Rocky is still attaching strands of wire to various bits of food to be used during the dining hall scene. To the casual viewer, it appears that he’s getting ready for a very unusual fishing expedition.

12:35 PM. Several grips lift the star drive onto a blue covered turntable in front of the blue screen. Footage taken during the previous OB filming is played back and composited over the turntable shot. With a few minor adjustments, it appears that the crew are standing around the device.

The star drive is switched on and its top section begins to whirl. By lowering the camera, the device (in the center of the shot) seems to rise, and as the camera tracks to the right, the star drives jumps out of frame.

12:50 PM. Scene 30. The crew are grouped around a star drive, bolting it to the floor. The drive thrums into life and then takes on a life of its own finally aiming straight for the boys.

The unit is reactivated, and Mel Bibby lies down on the floor, spinning the turntable manually to make the drive unit “hover” in place. Within a few minutes, Andy has his shot.

12:55 PM. The director walks over to the food table, where members of the FX team are still busy wiring up bits of food. “How are we doing over here?” he asks. Peter and Nick demonstrate some of the rigged food, which have been attached to long, fishing rod-like poles. Rocket walks over to tell Andy they need to do a film shot of the crew members in the cockpit.

The cast returns to the cockpit set, where Wragg will supervise the next shot. Unlike the other scenes which are shot on video, Peter needs a shot on film, which he hopes to composite into a model shot of Starbug. While other SF series have done such composite shots in the past, it's an adventurous thing to attempt on *Red Dwarf's* minuscule FX budget. The shot only takes a few minutes, and the crew breaks for lunch.

Lost scenes: Legion's banquet scene.

RIMMER: You have a connoisseur chip?

KRYTEN: Mandatory in all mechanoids, since the infamous Louvre incident, when a five hundred series prototype went cleansing crazy and scrubbed clean the Mona Lisa with a wire brush and sugar soap. Terrible business. Literally wiped the smile off her face.

...

1:45 PM. From lunch to a much more unusual meal. Simon and Andy are seated at Legion's dining table while Peter and his crew rehearse the dinner scene. Nick has constructed several sets of Mimosean anti-matter chopsticks: green Lucite devices that look like a DNA helix on a handle- which will figure heavily in the gags for this scene. Each chopstick is built with a small motor that allows them to rotate, and Nick checks each device to make sure it's in working order. Off to one side, FX assistant James Davis is working on a collapsible scalpel which will be used for a later scene.

2:30 PM. Scene 21A. The food and drink seems to have a life of its own, and only Kryten is able to utilize the anti-matter chopsticks. After several abortive attempts to partake of the goodies on offer, the table resembles the aftermath of a chimpanzees tea party!

The cast is brought into the dining hall set to begin work on what may be one of the most complicated scenes of season six. Robert's gloves are slipped on, and the tube leading to Nigel's mask is disconnected, although how Legion will eat through the tiny aperture is beyond me.

In the first part of the scene, Legion announces, "Let the meal begin." The boys pick up their chopsticks, without a clue as to how they're to be used.

Nigel tries to pick up his chopsticks, which proves difficult because of his mask. "Can you pick one of them up, Nigel?" directs Andy. A beat later: "Can you see them? Robert picks up his chopsticks. "I'm sorry, when do you want these turned on?" "Not in this shot," Andy tells him. It soon becomes evident that the chopsticks are going to be a problem. The tiny motors produce a tremendous whirring noise when they're working, which actually drowns out the dialogue. Nick later tells me that finding a noiseless motor would have wiped out a good part of the FX budget for that episode.

3:00 PM. The crew turn on their chopsticks with varying degrees of success. "This is where we want our first wire," Andy announces. Rocky brings in a small white, spidery-looking mass of food, and Peter extends a collapsible pole over it. A line is attached to the food so that it will appear to levitate into Legion's mouth.

Just as the cameras roll, one of Craig's chopsticks inexplicably falls apart. The crew roars with laughter. Apparently the life of any prop in Craig's possession is severely limited, and it's become a running joke on the Red Dwarf set. Nick rushes in to do some emergency surgery on the device.

"Right, let's do it again with food!" says Andy. While the actors leave the set, the next 20 minutes are spent doing shots of food floating into Legion's mouth. Unfortunately, most of them look like food hanging from a wire, and not very convincing.

Off-camera, the FX and props people prepare several identical meals for the shot where Rimmer gets splattered with food. The other actors take their places for the rest of the scene.

3:45 PM. A huge glop of green goo hits Chris in the side of his face, prompting another roar from the crew. Danny, who's sitting in the audience seating, well away from any actor/food contact, points to a monitor and announces, "That's funny!" For the next half hour, Chris is pelted by endless glops of food, to the delight of cast and crew.

4:20 PM. Chris leaves the set for a short rest while Craig and Nigel take their seats. This time it's Craig's turn to be deluged, when his glass of Mimosean telekinetic wine erupts into his face. The scene goes well, but as Craig leaves the set, he is reminded that for continuity reasons, he can't dry his shoulders.

Robert has an easier time with his scene. Since Kryten is supposed to be "willing" the wine from his glass to his mouth, all Robert has to do is squirt the liquid into his glass and run the tape backwards. The replay draws lots of laughs from the crew.

4:55 PM. Rimmer and the Cat fight over a piece of food which Rimmer has already swallowed. Every time he swallows it, the Cat's anti-matter chopsticks bring it up, stretching Rimmer's face out on one side. Obviously the effect will have to be augmented in post-production, but it's a funny scene to watch nonetheless.

5:30 PM. All actors are called back to the set for Rimmer's big speech, where he invites Legion to become a Dwarfer. While the actors rehearse, I take the opportunity to talk to producer Justin Judd. Earlier today, there were rumors that the next episode, 'Gunmen of the Apocalypse' has to be flip-flopped with the episode four, which is called 'Rimmerworld.' According to Justin, those rumors are true. "Here's one for the book," he says. "Because '*Gunmen'* was going to be so complicated to shoot, I made the decision to move episode four forward.

"We since discovered that episode four was every bit as complex as episode three. There's a note of irony for you!"

Back on set, Nigel has a question about a line in the script, and Justin and Bridget run off to find Rob and Doug. Andy decides to film the shot where Rimmer crosses the energy streams of his chopsticks and is pelted with food from every direction.

"Everybody ready?" the director asks. "We're only going to be able to do this once!" The scene goes off without a hitch, as Chris is struck with huge blobs of muck from six different directions.

As the crew breaks for dinner, I bump into Chris who's still covered with lumps of food. He smiles when I tell him the scene looked very funny. "It's really not that bad," he insists. "And now I have a warm shower to look forward to."

7:15 PM. Scene 24. Over breakfast, the boys discuss their escape plans. The set has been cleaned up, and the table reset with breakfast, champagne and orange juice. Having been told by Legion they will not be allowed to leave, the crew meets in the dining hall to decide what their next move will be. It's a very dialogue-heavy scene, and the cast has trouble running through their lines.

7:30 PM. Ready to record. Sure enough, it's a tough scene. On the first take, Chris and Robert step on each other's line, and on take two, Danny blows his "Who is this..." line. By the time Craig stumbles asking for another caviar nibblet, the pile of delicacies has gone down considerably. "If you miss a line," Simon finally cautions, "try to stumble through it as best you can.

Ten minutes later, Danny has blown the same line several times, and a frustrated Craig brandishes a bottle of bucks fizz in his direction. "If I have to eat any more caviar Dan, I'm going to pour this over your head!" he warns. A few minutes later, a full-of-caviar-and-bucks- fizz-Craig Charles delivers the final line. "That's the one," says Simon. While Craig goes off to change into his long johns, the set and costume people busy themselves dressing a statue in Lister's clothes. After drawing a crude face on it with a marker, the statue is ready for its big break in show business.

8:20 PM. Scene 26. As Legion enters the room, the boy smile falsely, hoping to gain his confidence. Lister's jacket is draped around the shoulders of a statue with its back to the door.

Nigel returns to the set, now with a strange- looking prosthetic makeup under his mask that makes him look like an amalgam of the four cast members. Although his face will actually be created by a computer effect, Andy wants the makeup for a brief shot where Legion's mask is dislodged.

While Chris, Danny and Robert remain seated, Craig stands behind the door, with a large piece of statuary hefted over his head. He's supposed do drop it on Legion who will deflect the attack with one arm, but loses his mask at the same time.

The scene is run several times, and after each take, Howard Burden has to step in and re-attach Legion's mask. Underneath it, Nigel is made up with Rimmer's H, a pair of Cat's teeth, and part of Kryten's mask

8:45 PM. Scene 26 (Con't). Legion throws Lister down the length of the table. He hits the wall and is rendered unconscious. Legion staggers in pain, and his face is now divided into thirds, Lister's having been eradicated.

Andy rehearses Nigel throwing Craig the length of the table. The effect is made easier by a small flat trolley the size of a skateboard which is placed under Craig's back to make him roll easier. As he slides across the table, Chris, Danny and Robert have to lift their dishes out of the way. Twenty minutes later, the same has to be shot again, this time with Danny making the trip.

9:50 PM. Scene 26 (Con't). Kryten attempts to eliminate Rimmer, but this can only be achieved by Rimmer turning off his own light bee.

With the 10 PM wrap time rapidly approaching, Andy asks the crew if they'll stay until the end of the scene. For this segment, Kryten tries to knock out Rimmer, only to discover that the hologram's new hard light drive is as tough as vindalooed mutton. He tells Rimmer that he'll render him unconscious with an Ionian nerve grip- and then smashes a vase over his head! On the second take, Robert goes to swing the vase over his head, but it slips from his grip and smashes to pieces. The tired crew cracks up, and the props master brings in a replacement vase.

10:15 PM. Robert continues to beat Chris over the head, first with a large serving tray, then a large piece of sculpture. Between takes, Chris checks the hologramatic H on his forehead to make sure it's still in place. The H, which a makeup assistant tells me is held on with two- sided toupee tape, has already been dislodged once or twice by the repeated blows to the head.

10:20 PM. With Rimmer now unconscious, Legion becomes an identical version of Kryten. That means the last sequence will have to be shot as a split screen, which will take some time. As I'm watching the scene, Bridget tells me my cab has arrived, so I make my good-byes. One crew member says he wished he could leave- the final scene still has to be finished.

Saturday, February 27. Audience Recording Day: 'Call Me Legion.'

10:00 AM. The day starts with rehearsals. Director and cast assemble around the table in the mid-section. Craig is dressed in jeans, windbreaker, stocking in cap and blue-tinted sunglasses. Robert in sweats. Danny is wearing a head kerchief, baggy pants, and a red flannel shirt Chris is dressed in jeans and a preppie blue sweater.

While the cast run through their lines, members of the crew are busy with an unusual task: trying to carve a carrot sculpture for tonight's opening scene. With several carrots standing by, everybody takes a try, with varying results. Steve Bradshaw's effort looks like one of the heads from Easter Island, while Rocky produces a carrot sculpture that looks more like a black-ribbed knobbler. The pile of carrots begins to shrink very quickly, while rejects continue to pile up.

Meanwhile, the finishing touches are being put on a set that will act as Lister's bedroom on the station. It's an interesting-looking set. A small bar against the wall is equipped with a bucket of chilled champagne. Above the refrigerator, an illuminated spinning clock. On one side of the bed is a round, pink and blue neon "Rock and roll" sign; on the other, a table topped by an antique radio and a small glass jar reading, "Danger- Dried Chillies." There's a vintage jukebox against one wall, over which the picture of a woman with the words "Babe Rainbow." Lying on the bed is a gleaming, chrome-plated guitar. The idea is this would be Lister's room, but channeled through Legion's eyes.

12:30 PM. It's time for the "stagger", where the cast goes through each of today's scenes in their respective sets. It starts with Rimmer and Kryten in the galley, and then moves on to Lister and the Cat in the cockpit

Nigel Williams enters the stage, dressed in civilian clothes, and sits down in the first row of audience seating. He only has one short scene tonight, so it's an easy day for him.

2:00 PM. The cast returns from lunch, and Andria grabs Chris to ask his opinion on next week's episode, 'Rimmerworld.' There's a scene in the script where Emperor Rimmer (played by Chris) kisses one of his lovely concubines (also played by Chris), and the production team is trying to decide the best way to shoot it. One suggestion is to superimpose Chris's face using blue screen, another; to put Chris in the concubine wig and makeup. Chris thinks it will look better and funnier with the wig, but Justin brings up the possibility of a time problem caused by an extra makeup change.

2:15 PM. Run-though of today's scenes. Because a large part of the episode has been pre-recorded, tonight's recording should go fairly smoothly.

4:15 PM. Scene 6. 'Psirens.' Kryten brings Rimmer to life via the computer. The crew sets up for a blue screen shot of Rimmer materializing in the opening scenes of Psirens. Rocket stands in for Chris to set up the shot.

5:05 PM. Chris comes in, dressed in his red uniform, standing motionless in front of the blue screen. As the camera rolls, he relives various memories, emotions, etc.

While Chris is shooting his scene, I spy former producer Paul Jackson (wearing his brand new Red Dwarf crew jacket) enter with his daughter. Although he's now the man in charge of Carlton

Television, Jackson still makes a point of attending a few recordings every season.

6:30 PM. Publicist Kate Cotton shows up, along with stills photographer Mike Vaughan. I tell Kate that if they want a photo of Legion, they're only going to get one chance. Since Mike wasn't present at the OB filming or the Pre-VT day, he'll have to get a shot of Nigel in costume during his one scene tonight. Neither Kate nor Mike were aware of that situation, and are grateful somebody took the time to tell them.

7:00 PM. The audience is allowed in, and the seats fill up very quickly. Meanwhile, the costume department checks with Andy to see if Legion is going to be introduced to the audience. They finally decide the best way to handle it is by sneaking him in through the side door just before his scene.

7:30 PM. The cast members are introduced to the audience, and the recording gets underway. The first live scene is with Kryten preparing a dinner of space weevil, much to Rimmer's displeasure. The weevil in question is an edible concoction prepared by Rocky, which looks very realistic and very disgusting. When Robert finishes the scene, he holds the plate out to the audience with a funny, TV commercial-type smile. He looks like he's shooting a late night infomercial.

9:05 PM. The live recording is finished early tonight, but warm-up man Andy Bull tells the audience they're welcome to stay and watch the re-shooting of a few scenes on the monitors. A few people leave. Most of them stay, and Danny entertains them by trying to ride Andy's unicycle- successfully, I should add.

9:15 PM. I go outside the stage for a cup of coffee, and sit down with Rob Grant and Production Manager Kerry Waddell who are sitting by the monitor. Rob usually chain-smokes his way through recordings, and there's already a small mountain of butts in the ashtray near his chair.

We're joined by Howard Burden, who's still a bit upset that he loaned his new pair of sneakers to Craig, for the scene where Lister removes them from the refrigerator in his cell. The sneakers hadn't even been worn before tonight, and now they're badly scuffed. So much for the glamour of show business.

Howard shows Rob a quick costume design for next week's Emperor Rimmer that he's sketched on the back of his script. The page is covered with small drawings, and Rob gives his approval to the final design.

Lost scenes: Lister's room. The final version of scene 22 ends with Lister strumming his guitar.

LISTER: Amazing. Doesn't even need tuning.

He takes a large handful from a bowl marked 'Danger- dried chilies' and starts to munch them like peanuts. He is suddenly seized by their super strength and starts to gag.

LISTER (When he can speak- impressed): Zippy chilies!

...

9:55 PM. With five minutes left before shutdown, the crew is trying to re-shoot part of scene 26, which was recorded on Thursday. The sequence in question is Kryten trying to knock out Rimmer using a marble statue. Looking back at the footage, Rob and Doug are less than happy with the scene, which is accompanied by unconvincing sound effects.

The "new" version has Kryten using a metal stanchion the size of a baseball bat, and repeatedly beating Rimmer over the head with it. Rob and Doug watch the re-shoot on the monitor, and are much happier with the final result. Out goes the statue, in comes the stanchion. After a few quick pickup shots for the dining hall scene, it's time to go home.

Tuesday March 2. OB Filming: 'Rimmerworld'/'Gunmen of the Apocalypse.'

2:00 PM. Scene 26. Rimmer gingerly tends a large egg. It cracks and a male Rimmer emerges.

It's a long day of OB filming, which started at 9:00 this morning, and will go until at least 10:00 tonight. Today's shooting schedule is divided between exteriors for this week's episode 'Rimmerworld' and the opening sequence for 'Gunmen of the Apocalypse.'

The first scenes of the day have already been recorded at Streeter Sand Quarry in Shepperton, showing Rimmer alone on top of a sand hill, where he surveys the barren Rimmerworld. The production team was only allowed to bring a minimal crew to the location, because the manager of the quarry didn't want too many people there.

James Davis (Visual FX)

What did you do with the egg?

James Davis: That was originally from The Alexei Sayle Show. We were lucky, because it was in stock storage, so it was just a matter of making it look as alien as possible. We could have made one exactly the right size, but would it have been worth it? In fact, I thought it was actually quite funny the way Rimmer is tending this egg that is quite huge, so you can save a lot of money on bits like that and put it towards other things. We textured it and painted it and made it more interesting on the inside with a little foam and painting it here and there.

...

*Lost scenes: Parts of Rimmer's narration was cut fr*om the aired episode:

RIMMER (VO): This is the personal log of Space Corps Hard Light Hologram, Arnold J. Rimmer, formerly of the Jupiter mining Corporation vessel, Red Dwarf. Day one. After a landing that would have won me full Bushito honors as a kamikaze pilot, I elected to venture forth to explore my new domain, and the place I would be calling home for the next two-thirds of a millennium.

Sandbank Near Chertsey (basically a big hill of sand): Camera at the bottom, we see RIMMER appear at the top. He picks up a handful of sand and lets it trickle through his fingers, then he scans the depressing terrain. He takes out his worry balls and starts to grind. Over all this we hear:

RIMMER (VO): A desert planet. The only life forms: the most basic *single-cell protozoa and me. Relationships would be difficult, but not impossible. I remembered the story of Alexander the Great. How, when he heard there were no worlds left to conquer, he broke down and wept. It gave me strength. I thought if it's OK for Alexander the Great, it's OK for me*

RIMMER is on his knees sobbing like a professional mourner.

RIMMER (VO): I sobbed like a child for nearly two hours. Afterwards, I felt strengthened and resolute, and decided to commit suicide immediately. But how? After much thought, I elected to shoot myself through the head with a flare gun. The attempt, of course, failed.

(The scene continues as aired)

…

The crew has now moved back into the Council Woods behind Shepperton Studios to shoot the birth of Rimmer's clone, as well as a later scene where Lister, Cat and Kryten are captured by Rimmer guards.

At the moment, we're standing in a wooded glade on the Shepperton back lot. A river flows through the area, with a narrow bridge running across it. Several yards away, a crumbling stone archway dominates the landscape. The area looks familiar, and one of the grips tells me that it was also used in last season's 'Terrorform.'

In one corner of the location, a giant egg is nestled against a clump of trees. Rocky, James and one of the props builders are busy getting it ready; adding wisps of cotton, and touching it up with spray paint. The egg was actually built for an episode of The Alexi Sayle show, but has been revamped for use in Red Dwarf.

Despite my heavy clothing, it's still very cold outside, but thanks to the skillful set dressers, it looks as if we're shooting in the middle of a lush spring meadow. Dozens of artificial flowers have been added to the vegetation, bringing it to life.

With the crew ready, Chris arrives and is put in position. The idea is that Rimmer has used the genetic seeding equipment on his escape pod to create a clone of himself; that's what is about to hatch from the egg. As Chris approaches the object, his voice-over describes the action taking place. A second take is ordered, then a third. Nobody is wasting time, as the crew tries to take advantage of the last few hours of good light on an overcast day.

"Can we open the egg, please?" requests Andy. A few feet away, Tim Fisher who is acting as Chris's double for the sequence, strips down and climbs into a dressing gown. Bare-footed, he pads across the glade and climbs into the open egg.

"The idea is that the egg cracks open," Andy explains to Chris, "you lean back this way, and then it's all done with the eyes- oh no, it's gone horribly wrong!" Tim is bundled into the egg which is re-sealed, and fresh wisps of cotton are placed over it.

2:30 PM. Ready to record. Rocky stands off-camera, a set of smoke canisters at the ready. The egg wobbles and cracks open. In the middle of the freezing cold glade, Tim stands up completely naked, and Chris looks at him, up...and then down. The voice-over announces, "Something had gone horribly wrong," and Chris's accompanying expression is priceless. The take is greeted with a spontaneous burst of applause, and after a close-up on Chris, Tim goes away to get dressed.

As the crew prepares for the next shot, some of them start poking fun at lighting director John Pomphrey, who fell into the water during the filming of 'Terrorform' last year. Like an elephant, a film crew never forgets, and the crew has even gone as far as placing a life preserver on the side of the lighting van with John's name on it. To his credit, he takes it all with good grace. "You can say in your book," he tells me, "that the only one who didn't fall in the water was the gaffer. He stayed warm and dry!"

Rocky packs the gas canisters back in their case. "They decided not to use them he explains, "because A) there's a naked man in there who psychologically might feel confined, and B) the smoke doesn't like to be confined."

Chris returns to the set wearing a robe, and is placed inside the egg so they can shoot another close-up. The egg's interior is lined with white foam, and is weighted down to keep it from moving. Simon calls for some people standing on the other side of the river to move, so they're not caught in the back of shot

3:00 PM. For the reverse shot, Chris rises out of the egg with his robe pulled down to his waist, and gives an innocent smile. "Very good, but we need to do one without the breathing," says Andy, referring to the telltale vapor trailing from Chris's mouth. On the third take, Rocky and James open the egg, and Chris rises from it, smiling and blinking like an innocent child. "That's the one!" the director announces.

3:15 PM. Scene 31. Lister, Cat and Kryten meet Rimmer Roman guards. The crew moves several hundred yards away, into another clearing. Ron Green the gaffer tells me this area was recently used in the short-lived Covington Cross. Rocky and James start spreading smoke from their canisters, and within minutes, we're surrounded by a low-hanging mist.

3:30 PM. Craig, Danny and Robert enter the glen dressed in their costumes. Craig and Danny are wearing heavy coats, and one of the dressers carefully places a coat over Robert's head and shoulders. Andy asks the FX men to try blowing smoke in from a lower angle.

Chris arrives in the glen, dressed in a Roman/medieval costume and maroon types. He salutes the other cast members standing nearby, and Robert shouts, "Hail to the chief!

Rina stands a few feet in front of me with a large cue card, and Simon calls for rehearsal. A props man hands Chris a long spear, and the rest of the cast laughs, making a few suggestive remarks at their costar's expense.

On the first take, Chris is supposed to step out behind the other three. He leaps out, brandishes his spear and shouts, "Silence mutants!" The other cast member double over with laughter, and even Chris loses his composure, realizing how silly he looks to everyone.

Meanwhile, Chris's double Tim has been re-costumed as a Roman guard, along with two other extras. It's very cold out, but Tim doesn't seem to notice. "Did you see me earlier?" he asks, still excited about his Red Dwarf debut. Ironically, fans will never see his face in either scene today, because he's playing a Rimmer clone.

4:00 PM. The scene starts rolling, but is interrupted by a low-flying plane. Andy calls for more smoke, and they start again. Craig, Danny and Robert re-enter the glen. Robert is wearing a futuristic backpack and carrying a psi- scan. Danny is dressed in the same black trousers as the previous episodes, but with a black leather jacket trimmed in orange. The first take goes okay.

The three Roman doubles are brought in and put in position. Meanwhile the crew is standing around reciting lines from Julius Caesar, including Chris who's definitely dressed for the part. John Pomphrey looks up at the sky, worrying about the amount of available light. "We're going to be struggling to finish this," he says quietly.

4:10 PM. The scene is rehearsed again. Cast members are still wearing their coats although Roman guards are not. "Okay, can we get them undressed and go for a take on this, please?" asks Andy. Dressers rush in, removing coats and adjusting costumes. The scene is then shot, with the three guards and Rimmer escorting their prisoners through the woods.

In order to finish the scene, Chris is re-positioned in the place of the three guards. By cutting these close-ups together with long shots of the guards, it will appear that all four soldiers have Rimmer's face. The scene is finished just after 5 PM. Chris and Danny are released for the day, but Craig and Robert are needed for the night shoot.

7:00 PM Scene 5 'Gunmen of the Apocalypse.' Kryten appears as a gangster. Lister continues snogging, but is eventually persuaded to return to reality.

The crew is busily setting up for the gangster sequences of 'Gunmen' in the dock area behind Shepperton. At the beginning of the episode, Kryten has to enter an artificial reality game, where Lister is role-playing as a gangster. By the time Kryten shows up, his companion is "occupied" with a lovely femme fatale in the back of a steamed up car. Craig stands off to one side, dressed in a gangster suit, with his shirt un-tucked. His costar is Jennifer Calvert, who's appeared in such programs as Brookside and Spatz . She too is dressed in period clothing, looking like she just stepped out of Sam Spade's office in The Maltese Falcon.

Nearby, Robert is wearing a pin-striped suit and hat, with a mustache pasted over his Kryten mask. He is very happy to be dressed in a comfortable suit instead of the restrictive costume. "It halves the discomfort," he says with some relief. Against a brick wall is parked a vintage black automobile (a '39 Packard?). The crew is busy trying to dull the shine of the car so it won't pick up any reflections from the lights. Two ripple tanks have been placed a few yards away, to make it appear that the car is parked next to water. An old street light has been erected to complete the illusion.

These scenes by the way, are going to be shot in black and white, and looking at a nearby monitor, the set looks very impressive. Craig and Jennifer are asked to get in the car, and Craig asks for a mint before his big scene. Andy, standing in front of the monitor, calls for smoke. Ron Green starts stirring the water in one tank to create ripples, which are reflected onto the car and wall. "Lots of smoke, please!" calls Andy.

7:45 PM. First shot of the night, as Kryten materializes in the AR game. The effect is done simply by filming the empty frame, stopping the camera, and having Robert step into the appropriate place.

"Can we steam the car windows now?" asks Andy, and Rocky gets into the car, spraying the windows from the inside. The door is closed, and several stage hands start rocking the car gently from side to side. Robert stands next to the car, bright lights reflecting off his polished black shoes. "He's doing his own rocking," he quips of Craig's activities inside the car. "He does all his own stunts, and all his own rocking!" Simon calls for the car to be rocked a bit harder.

7:55 PM. Robert stands near the front of the car, a violin case under his right arm. He now wears black gloves. "Cue Robert!" He walks up to the rocking car, attempts to

wipe the moisture off one of the windows with his glove but can't see a thing. He knocks briskly on the window. After a second take, the shot is in the can.

8:05 PM. The cameras are moved, and John Pomphrey readjusts his lights accordingly. "I love black and white," be comments. "It's so evocative!" Five minutes later, they're ready to shoot. Robert knocks on the window again. A disheveled Craig peers out. After the third take, he gets out of the car to check the shot on a monitor. Robert leans against the car, looking as casual as a mechanoid dressed in gangster clothing can look, I suppose.

8:45 PM. Close-up on Kryten. Andy calls for more smoke, but to everyone's surprise, a huge cloud of steam vents from the neighboring building. The FX boys are as surprised an anyone else.

9:15 PM. Scene 1. 1940's gangster/moll setting, where Lister greets Loretta. Jennifer stands under the streetlight, holding two suitcases. She puts her bags down, and the Bentley roars up, stopping a few feet away.

Craig, now wearing a long coat over his suit, walks up to me. "What do you think?" he asks, proudly displaying his choice in evening wear. Not bad, I tell him. "Is this about the naked, unvarnished Red Dwarf, then?" a reference to my book. Diplomacy is obviously the order of the day, and I say I'm just reporting what I see- within reason of course. Fortunately, Craig is called back to the set, saving me from further questioning.

As the crew records a shot of the car pulling up, John Pomphrey and Jeff Jeffrey the technical manager worry about a series of tiny sparks showing up on camera, which may be coming from the car. They discover that the sparks seem to stop once the car is shut off, and the shot is finished without incident.

Then it's time to shoot the car approaching from a distance. Andy thinks the area is too bright and the headlights won't show up properly. "John, can we lose a little of the light on that wall?" he asks the lighting director. After a few adjustments, the shot goes OK.

9:45 PM. Scene 3. Lister and Loretta continue kissing. The scene that Craig has been waiting for: the big, long- delayed kiss. After suffering through five loveless seasons and endless lobbying with the writers, Lister finally gets a big love scene, and he's making the most of it. After a rehearsal kiss, costume and makeup step in to make a few touch-ups and they're ready to roll.

Craig decides to do his lines Bogart style with a cigarette in his mouth, which turns out not to be a good idea. "I don't think we can keep that cigarette in your mouth the whole time," warns Andy. "We're losing some of the words." On the next take, Craig takes a dramatic puff and then lowers the cigarette. It works much better. The next take is a bit too dramatic. "It's a bit John Wayne- y there," the director comments, prompting a roar of laughter from the crew.

After the next take and a final kiss, Craig looks directly into the camera, with the happiest, shit-eating grin imaginable. His mouth and face are covered with lipstick, but he's a happy man.

10:05 PM. All that's left are the last few angles to cover. The final clinch is interrupted by a pair of low-flying ducks, who loudly announce their presence as they swoop over our heads. "Just coming back from the pub!" someone jokes. Ten minutes later, the last shot is finished, and it's time to return to our nice warm homes.

Thursday, March 4. Pre-VT Day: 'Rimmerworld.'

10:00 AM. It's always strange to come in on a Thursday morning, and see the new sets for the next episode. This time, Mel's team has constructed Emperor Rimmer's throne room; a strange amalgam of

Roman and Egyptian styles. It's filled with ivy-covered pillars and feathered fans, all on an imitation marble floor. A raised Egyptian throne is flanked by a pair of jackal statues, with a large round H symbol hanging behind it.

Directly across from the throne room set is Rimmer's escape pod, a large, man-sized gray chamber, that looks like a cross between an electric chair and a high-tech phone booth. On one counter is a spiral-bound "Genetic Cloning Manual." The pod has been built by nearby Vendetta FX, who created the chamber out of spare parts within a few days.

John Pomphrey walks up behind me. "I think it was Danny yesterday who said every home should have one," he says, indicating the pod. Just put it in and you have everything right there- hi-fi; everything!"

10:20 AM. Scene 12. The cast assembles in the midsection to meet themselves. The Week-Last-Thursday crew is seated for the first part of the split screen sequence. After a quick rehearsal, makeup moves in for a quick adjustment and they're ready to record.

"Okay, you're busy checking your papers, Craig," instructs Andy. "Danny, you're checking your buttons and talking to Kryten." The scene is shot, followed by various close-ups, and then a "clean frame" of just the set.

10:45 AM. Robert is filled with his futuristic backpack to show that he is from the future. Peter hands him the psi- scan and teleporter.

11:05 AM. It's time to shoot the future Starbug crew materializing on the ship. The cast is arranged in a different position around the mid-section, and when both elements are combined with an electronic effect, the shot will be complete.

11:45 AM. Scene 13. The cast is seated around the mid-section table playing cards without Lister. This scene is followed by Lister's entrance, followed by the closing lines.

*Lost scenes: The original ending for 'Rimmerworld was significantly longer than t*he one that aired:

OTHER VERSION OF RIMMER: Rimmerworld was weeks ago. We're far more concerned at the moment with the quite hideous thing that's happened to Lister.

CAT: He's right. Where are you, Bud?

LISTER: Yeah, where am I?

KRYTEN: Sir, we've seen too much already. We really must be going.

KRYTEN punches the console and they begin to dematerialize.

LISTER: What happened to me? I've got to know!

They disappear. Small pause. We hear a toilet flush, and other version of LISTER steps out of the rear door.

OTHER VERSION OF LISTER: What was that? I thought I heard voices.

OTHER VERSION OF RIMMER: Voices? Don't think so, Listy. You must have imagined it. Your deal.

OTHER VERSION OF RIMMER starts dealing the cards, obvious.

OTHER VERSION OF KRYTEN (To OTHER VER*SION OF RIMMER): You've learned nothing, have you? One might almost be tempted to conclude you truly are irredeemable, undiluted moral slime.*

RIMMER: We try, Kryten, we try.

(The credits roll)

…

2:15PM. The crew gets ready to shoot in the Emperor's throne room. These scenes will be just as difficult as the earlier split screen, because several Rimmers have to be placed in the same shot. By using a combination of appropriately dressed doubles and several splits with Chris, the scenes will be together like jigsaw puzzles in the editing.

Chris enters the set, dressed as the Emperor. He has a voluptuous concubine on each arm, their faces covered with veils. The joke is that both of these sexy women will have Rimmer's face. The concubines are dressed in Roman/Egyptian costumes, with gauzy skirts, jeweled breast plates, golden sandals and Cleopatra-like headdresses. They're also wearing snake-shaped armbands, which Howard Burden asks one of his assistants to adjust in order to give them greater visibility.

Four Roman guards are positioned around the set. They're glad to finally be doing something, having sat around their dressing room for the last few hours in costume, waiting for this scene. Howard's assistant Gill Shaw brings in Craig's heavy coat for him to put on. This scene is a carry-over from the previous OB sequence, where the Starbug crew is captured by Rimmer guards.

A stagehand tapes the lip of the "marble" tiled floor, so the cameras can roll over it without pulling up the tiles.

Rocket points to Chris, who is standing near the entrance. "Excuse me, your Emperor-ness, can you piss off and come in right? Far from being a rude remark, it's Rocket-speak for Chris to go out and come back in again from the right side of the set.

"Can I have Danny in?" asks Rocket. Although the Cat isn't actually in shot, the cameraman needs him to frame the shot. He then tells Andy that there is a big gap between Chris and the concubines. The entrance will have to be reduced in some way.

2:30 PM. We're ready for the Emperor's big entrance. With a crescendo of terrible Hammond organ music, the concubines walk into the throne room, followed by Chris. "Do we have a longer version of the music?" Andy inquires. The actors return to their marks for the next take. [Ironically, the entrance will never be used. In the final cut of Rimmerworld , Chris is nearly seated when the prisoners are brought in]

Lost scenes: The original throne room entrance:

LISTER, CAT and KRYTEN are led in by the RIMMER GUARDS (stand-ins in long shot) Might be nice to have another two RIMMER GUARDS standing either side of the door.

CASTLE HALL: Again, the same kind of Roman Emperor/ Medieval chieftain hybrid. Two RIMMER GUARDS either side of the throne.

LISTER, KRYTEN, CAT and GUARD ONE enter. An OILED RIMMER bangs a gong.

OILED RIMMER: Pray silence for His Most Excellent Majesty.

FIRST RIMMER GUARD: Stand to attention, mutant scum, while they play the anthem.

Truly awful Hammond ORGAN music, complete with glis*sandos and Bosa Nova rhythm unit, plays in EMPEROR RIMMER, who wears an 'H' on his head, flanked by two voluptuous CONCUBINES, wielding large palms for fanning purposes.*

All the OTHER RIMMERS do the Rimmer Salute. EMPEROR RIMMER returns it.

EMPEROR RIMMER: Who disturbs our royal snooze?

(Scene continues as written)

...

Directly across from the throne room, Craig is resting on one of the bunks in sleeping quarters. Since he's not actually in the shot from this angle, he shouts his lines from the other set.

2:40 PM. Robert and Craig are brought back to the set to record their take. Torches are lit near the back of the set. Robert's backpack is put on, and they're ready to go

"Heads down, everyone," instructs Simon. The Rimmer guards each bow their heads obediently. Emperor Rimmer enters and takes his place on the throne. The Rimmer guards salute.

3:00 PM. With the various elements of Rimmer's entrance shot, it's time to shoot the remaining Emperor shots. These takes are particularly tedious for Chris, because of their technical nature, as well as the need to keep each take fresh.

4:30 PM. Now for the other side of the shot, showing Lister, Cat and Kryten. Between takes, Andria and assistant Lois Burwell get ready to re-glue Robert's mask down around his eyes. It's a very sensitive procedure, which the usually placid Robert hates with a passion. He later tells me it's because his entire face become numb after a few hours, except for the bags around his eyes, which become hyper-sensitive. Confronted with the glue brushes, Robert begins to complain loudly. "Okay, wait a minute," he finally says, and screams loudly. Everyone on the set turns around, thinking perhaps a heavy lamp has fallen on Robert's head. "Okay, do it," he says resignedly.

Liz Hickling, who will be playing a rogue simulant later this afternoon, comes in as excited as a small child to be working on Red Dwarf. She goes to see Howard about her costume.

Andria, who's just finished working on Robert's mask, tells me that they'll placing bits of computer wire around Liz's face. Her character will actually be seen in 'Gunmen' first, which shoots next week, and when she returns in 'Rimmerworld,' it's in a badly damaged state. To that end, damaged pieces of machinery will be protruding from various places in her face and body.

5:10 PM. A few crew members start setting up for the scenes in the engine room set, which has been partially redressed as part of the crumbling simulant ship. Wragg's FX team hoists a load of fake debris, where it will eventually fall on the simulant's head.

The set now consists of several large crates, a large metal contraption with several gadgets that look like railroad switches, and a small device mounted against one wall. The machine is fitted with a blinking red light and a digital timer which reads :18. Written in raised letters are the words "Macdyne Alba Teleport, and another readout indicates the machine is in "Roam Mode."

Opposite the device is oversized square platform bordered with florescent lights. It looks like a miniature disco dance floor. Apparently this is the teleport pad, and the machine; the teleporter itself.

Meanwhile, Andy discusses the use of a new weapon with Peter. It's a futuristic rifle which attaches to the owner's arm. A hinge allows it to swing down and lock into place. The reason for such a unique weapon is because the simulant has lost an arm in the partial destruction of her ship, and this gun only requires one arm to use.

While the crew is setting up, I chat with Alison Marsh, one of the twins who play Rimmer's concubines. They usually work as singers, who have traveled all over the world. They're currently writing songs for a Japanese music publisher, as well their faceless (and uncredited) appearance in Red Dwarf.

5:30 PM. The final sequence in the throne room has Rimmer kissing "himself." Chris is made up with a glamour makeover, which leads to plenty of good natured ribbing from the crew. A veil is placed over his face, to get a close-up of the Rimmer concubine, and finally Rebecca Marsh's face is seen from the side as she kisses Chris. The take is a source of great merriment to the crew. Simon asks Andy, "Can I release the concubines?"

Alison Marsh (Concubine)

How did you and Rebecca end up coming in to do these parts?

Alison Marsh: They wanted twins, and we're known as twins in the business, and so we went for an audition, and they called us up just to do this little bit here. They originally wanted us for a speaking part, but that changed, and then they wanted us to do this.

What sort of things do you normally do?

Marsh: We're singers mainly. We write our own music, but obviously the twin thing is quite unique.

Do you play that up to your advantage?

Marsh: Oh yeah, we use it when it's required. We normally only do things where we're featured, but Andy liked us and asked us if we'd mind coming in to do this. It's just a day's work, plus it's a great series. I think it's very well-written, and very intellectual compared to a lot of the comedies around now.

…

7:00 PM. Scene 7. Crew explores the simulant ship. The cast reassembles in the simulant ship set. Chris is now wearing a hard light projection belt, and is carrying a pair of Japanese worry balls given to him earlier in the story by Kryten.

According to the script, they've boarded the derelict simulant ship looking for salvage. They find a working teleporter, which they use to transport cargo onto Starbug, but an encounter with a remaining simulant alters their plans. The FX men fill the chamber with smoke, and they're ready to start.

8:45 PM. The crew meet a very angry rogue simulant. In order to simulate the ship shaking apart, the camera is jiggled; a simple and convincing effect.

Liz Hickling is made up as the damaged simulant. She's dressed in a black body suit with one arm tied behind her and wires protruding from the torn sleeve. She's also wearing a headpiece which was once worn by the killer droid in 'Justice.' Before shooting, Andy has a discussion with costume and makeup on how to make the headpiece more convincing. "It's a bit stuck on, isn't it?" he asks them. A few more wires are added to make it look more damaged.

9:15 PM. Rimmer escapes into pod. At the far end of the set is a sliding door with a green and red lit panel over it. It reads "Escape Pod 736." A blinking yellow alert light hangs from the ceiling in front of it.

Chris punches a code into the keypad, and the door opens. He steps inside, the door slides shut, and the words "Pod Launched" blink on.

After the take, the costume and makeup people make a few adjustments to Liz's headpiece. Using a pair of wire cutters, some of the protruding filaments are cut off and twisted. It doesn't look very different.

Paul McGuiness blows smoke back into the set, which spreads very quickly. The cameras roll again, and the third take ends with a pile of fake debris falling on the simulant.

9:45 PM. Andy needs a shot of Chris punching a code into the keypad in order to open the pod door. The actor talks to the stage hands on the other side of the door, telling them how many lights he'll punch in before they open the door.

The last shot of the night is Lister, Cat and Kryten teleporting out of exploding ship. The actors step on the raised platform, and after a shot of them standing on it, they step out of frame and the camera is locked off so the teleportation effect can be added in post-production.

As Simon calls a wrap for the night, I notice Liz Hickling standing a few yards away. Clad only in her black body suit, her arm has been released from the constrictive tunic. She stretches happily, like a cat in front of a fireplace. When we see her next week, she'll be a healthy simulant again.

Saturday, March 6. Audience Recording Day: 'Rimmerworld.'

10:00 AM. While the cast is rehearsing today's scenes, I take Jeff Jeffrey up on his offer of a tour of the facilities. In order to write a true behind-the-scenes account of Red Dwarf he tells me, I have to the technical elements that go into it.

11:45 AM. Back in Stage G, the set constructed for tonight's recording is Rimmer's prison cell. It features a straw-covered floor, a heavy wooden door, a simulated stone walls. One wall is covered by white chalk marks, which indicate the passage of time. Since the entire wall is covered by these marks, it's easy to see that a considerable amount of time has passed.

Next to the wall is a small, rickety wooden bed, covered by a sackcloth blanket. It is here that the boys discover their lost companion, who's been imprisoned for more than six centuries.

12:30 PM. The cast assemble in the cell to rehearse the penultimate scene. Chris is covered by the blanket, and toys with a vastly-reduced pair of worry balls. These are the size of ball bearings, indicating a good deal of rubbing over the years.

2:00 PM. Rehearsals continue, but by this time, the cast has got a bit punchy. First, Danny cuts off Robert's line about the number of years marked on the cell wall. "I haven't counted them yet!" laughs Robert.

The rehearsals continue, with much laughter and missed lines. Word comes down that Rob and Doug have arrived and someone remarks, "Now that the producers have arrived, maybe we should look interested!"

2:15PM. Stagger-through. The cast runs through each of tonight's scene in order, starting with Chris and Robert in the ops room. Robert is wearing a stethoscope around his neck, prompting a few "Dr. Kryten" jokes from the crew.

2:30 PM. "I'm getting the smell of something burning here," says Craig, who's sitting in the cockpit. "Is it ham?' comes the response from where the writers are sitting. The look on Craig's face is priceless. It turns out to be Danny's peanuts from last week's episode, which have fallen onto one of the lamps and started cooking.

4:10 PM. After a short break, the cast resume rehearsals. By this time, Robert is in makeup, and Chris is wearing his blue hard light uniform.

7:30 PM. Audience recording. Tonight's taping goes relatively well, although the opening scene between Robert and Chris takes some time to get through.

It's interesting to watch how the four cast members react in front of a live audience. Craig frequently plays to the audience, joking and speaking directly to them. Robert does the same thing to a lesser extent, although he frequently stays in character. His Kryten's Granddad routine is an audience favorite, and Craig often sets him up for a quick routine.

In contrast, Danny takes the recordings much more seriously than he does rehearsals. It's not uncommon to see him sail through rehearsals with only a passing understanding of the script. When he steps in front of the camera however, his stage training takes over and he becomes a total professional.

Of course there are exceptions. When Danny forgets a line, a blank look crosses his face, followed by the innocent smile of a boy caught with his hand in the cookie jar. Case in point: during tonight's recording, during a scene where Rimmer is told it will take 600 years for Starbug to pick him up. "Six hundred years?" asks the shocked Rimmer. Danny's gag line: "Pinch me!" but he misses it completely. A few seconds later, there's that bashful grin!

Finally, there's Chris. Easily the most professional of the lot, he hates blowing a line and rarely speaks directly to the audience. When someone else misses their line, his expression is that of a patient adult taking three mischievous teenagers on a field trip. On the rare occasions that he lets his hair down with a joke or one of his funny, letter-perfect impressions, the audience cheers loudly.

When tonight's recording is over, I head for home instead of the pub where most of the cast and crew gather for a drink. Next week will be a busy one.

Tuesday, March 9. OB Filming: 'Gunmen of the Apocalypse.'

8:15 AM. The crew starts filtering in to the streets of the Laredo Western Club in Kent, where today's location filming for 'Gunmen' will be taking place.

Several crew members are already hard at work. On one end of the street, the FX crew is hanging up a bogus "You are now leaving Existence sign," which will be rigged to fall later in the day. The set dressers are also busy adding finishing touches to the facades of different buildings. Their work has been made considerably by members of the club, who have worked very hard to make their village as authentic-looking as possible.

One by one, I start to see members of the cast, now dressed in official Red Dwarf cowboy garb. Chris is in a gray outfit, a long tan coat, and a gray cowboy hat. Craig is wearing a black jacket, hat and gloves, while Robert as sheriff Kryten is dressed in a beat-up old coat, brown pants, white shirt and a scarf which hides the bottom of his mask. He's also wearing an extra-large cowboy hat to fit over the mask.

Danny rides up on a white horse, grinning broadly (Danny, not the horse). He's dressed in a black Spanish cowboy outfit trimmed in silver and a matching sombrero. He looks like he should be the forth Amigo, from the film featuring Martin Short, Steve Martin and Chevy Chase, but hopefully much funnier. While Danny is obviously quite comfortable on horseback, the other cast members aren't. Chris looks decidedly nervous about the idea, but Craig doesn't hesitate. He jumps onto the back of another horse, and one of the trainers gives him a quick riding lesson.

After his equine tutorial, Craig dismounts, and walks over to where Chris and I are standing. He looks like a big happy kid. The two cast members compare guns, and I start to feel inadequate: all I've got is a clipboard and a big pen.

It's a gorgeous sunny day- too gorgeous in fact. The sun is so bright that the first shot of the day has to be changed to a shadier spot. "How often does that happen in England in mid-March?" asks one of the crew.

The four horseman ride into town and are positioned in front of the livery building at the far end of the block. Three of the actors are unfamiliar to me, but I recognize Denis Lill from his work in Survivors and Doctor Who. Denis is playing a dual role in this episode; he'll be appearing as the Simulant Captain on Thursday. Rina offers him his chewing tobacco for the day- actually licorice. Somehow I don't think John Wayne or Gary Cooper chewed licorice, but this is England so I keep my mouth shut.

Simon asks the horsemen to re-position themselves in front of the saloon a few hundred yards away. Robert is called in, and he removes his coat. He stands underneath the Last Chance Saloon sign, staggering around and looking drunk. Because the mask conceals so much of his facial expression, Robert uses broad body language, much like the legendary silent film comics.

As Kryten gets ready to confront the Four Horsemen, I see one of the extras standing off to the right filming the scene on his own camcorder. The sight of a man dressed in realistic western garb looking through a brand new video camera is an unsettling one. The day is peppered with little incidents like that.

Lost scenes: The original version of Kryten's encounter with the Four Horsemen:

Outside the saloon, the cowboy version of THE FOR HORSEMEN OF THE APOCALYPSE wait on their mounts, leaning casually on their saddles.

KRYTEN: Who's askin' for the sheriff, friend?

DEATH: The name's Death. And these here's my brothers. Brother War…

WAR laughs and flames shoot out of his mouth.

DEATH: Brother Famine…

FAMINE touches the brim of his hat with his hand. It is a skeleton.

DEATH: And Brother Pestilence.

PESTILENCE grins. Horrible broken teeth, he swipes idly at the swarm of buzzing flies around his head.

KRYTEN: You seem like a right neighborly bunch of boys. How can your friendly sheriff help you?

DEATH: See now, Brother Pe*stilence here has a problem. Seems you're standing right exactly where his bullets want to be.*

WAR laughs and bellows flames.

KRYTEN: Oh, I'm sorry.

KRYTEN shuffles to one side.

KRYTEN: This more accommodating?

DEATH shakes his head.

DEATH: Well, ain't that just the darndest thing? Now you're standing exactly where my bullets want to be.

KRYTEN: Oh, I uh…

KRYTEN shuffles to the other side.

DEATH: Is that OK for you, Brother War?

WAR shakes his head sadly. KRYTEN moves further along.

DEATH: Brother Famine?

FAMINE shakes his head.

KRYTEN: I'm really not having much luck, am I?

KRYTEN moves again.

DEATH (sighs): I got to figure you're doing this just to plain provoke me.

ALL FOUR APOCALYPSE BOYS draw, shoot KRYTEN'S hat off, his bottle out of his hand, his gun belt drops to the floor, and he dances around, trying to avoid the hail of bullets. Finally, the gunfire stops. KRYTEN'S clothes are in tatters.

KRYTEN: What do you want of me?

DEATH: I want your sorry ass out of her, Sheriff. You got till the final stroke of midnight.

THE FOUR HORSEMEN turn and rid off. They pass a dangling sign: 'You are now leaving Existence.'

...

9:30 AM. Craig and I enter the Assay and Registry office, which we think is an empty storefront. To our surprise, the room is occupied by two elderly members of the Laredo Western Club, who invite us in and offer us coffee. The two cowpokes are named John and A.J., and their little hideaway is a perfect recreation of a 19th century store. Our coffee is brewed in an ancient black coffee pot, on top of a cast iron stove that fills the small room with warmth. Despite the heat, I suddenly experience a chill, as though I've just gone back in time. Craig seems unaffected.

Scene 31. Sheriff Kryten encounters the Four Horsemen of the Apocalypse. They show their dislike for him by shooting at his whiskey bottle, hat and gun belt, followed by a further hail of bullets. They warn him to be out of town by midnight.

Outside, a hatless Robert is holding a broken bottle in one hand; destroyed by the gunmen. As the desperadoes continue shooting, the FX boys use compressed air guns to fire pellets of colored dust at the ground. The effect simulates the dust kicked up by real bullets, but it proves to be too much for one of the horses. It throws Robert (War) Inch to the ground while the other horses appear less than happy. After a few seconds of confusion, the horsemen (and their horses) are back in position in front of the saloon.

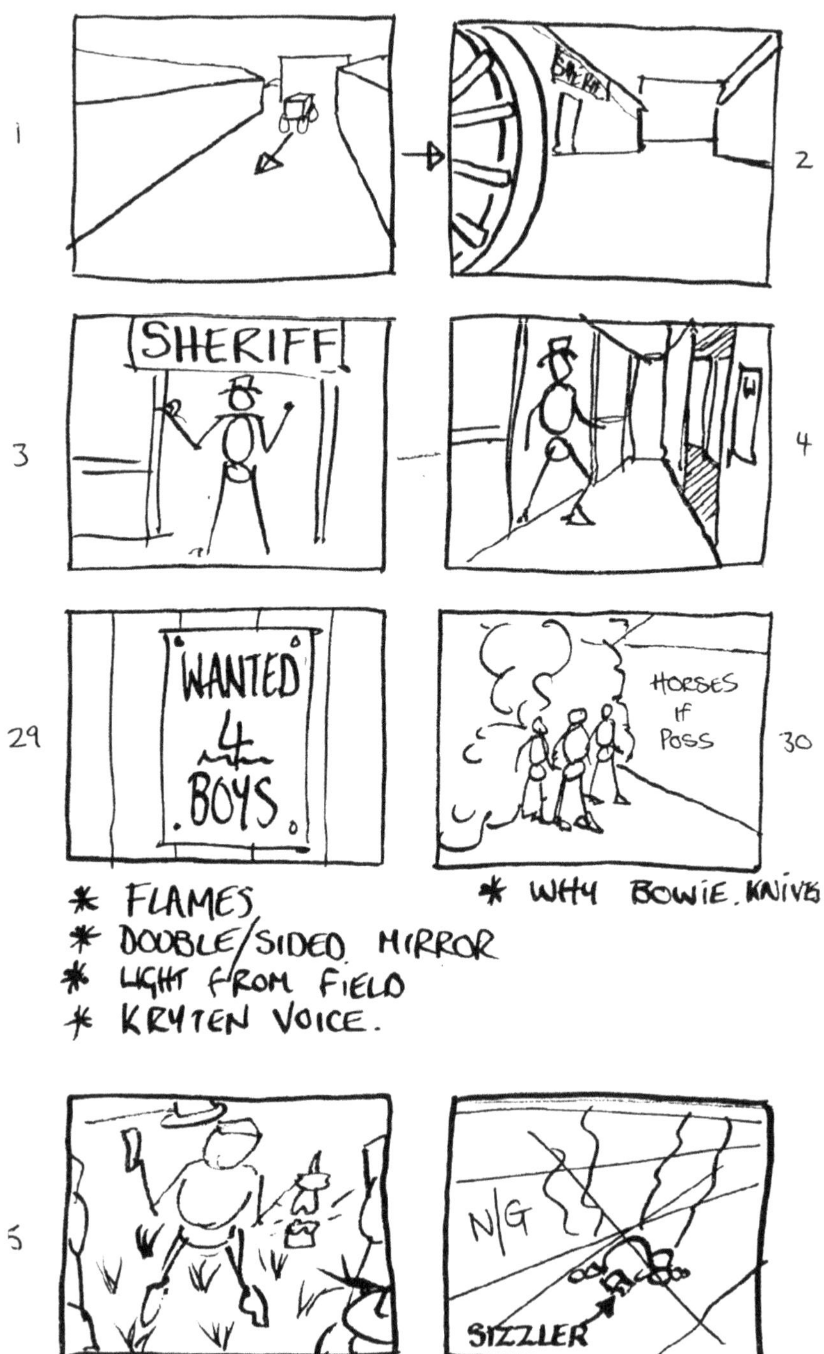

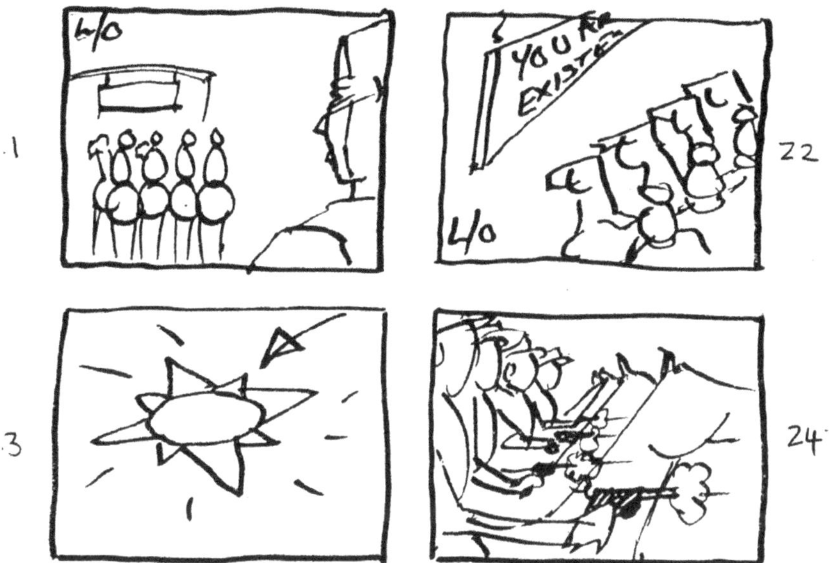

Director Andy DeEmmony's rough storyboards for 'Gunmen.'

A few words about the Last Chance Saloon: it's a two- story building, with a sign on the top floor reading "P.J. Cobbs General Store." One of the sound men stands on the landing holding the boom mike. Below, a sign advertises the Last Chance Saloon. A wanted poster has been tacked onto one of the beams, reading "Wanted Dead or Alive: The Four Apocalypse Boys."

The Horsemen are positioned for their individual close-ups. They make an interesting sight. Pestilence (Jeremy Peters) is wearing a sickly, sunken-in makeup, covered with peeling skin. He waves his hand as if to shoo away a cloud of flies, which will be added in postproduction.

Death (Denis Lill) has a big black mustache and weather-beaten features. He looks like the archetypical western bad guy. War (Robert Inch) is dressed like a civil war deserter, with a well-worn blue jacket and buckskin pants. His makeup consists of a thick black eyebrow that goes across his forehead like a runaway caterpillar.

Finally, there's Famine (veteran stunt man Dinny Powell) He's a big, burly guy (thanks to heavy padding courtesy of Howard Burden and Co.) and wears a black patch over one eye. For his close-up, he brandishes a half-eaten chicken leg at the camera.

Andy requests a torch for War, who's supposed to breath a stream of fire. "Can we get a mouthful first," asks Inch. He takes a heavy swig of paraffin from a Styrofoam cup, and someone hands him the torch. He blows an impressive plume of fire, but Andy isn't quite happy with it; the flames are difficult to see in the bright sunlight. Subsequent takes become difficult because the horse is still skittish, but a second take goes well.

Meanwhile, the "locals" mix with the other cast members not in shot. Cameras are produced, photos are taken, autographs are signed- lots of them. For members of the Laredo Western Club, this is probably the most exciting thing to happen to their little cowboy community in years.

10:25 AM. A new bottle is filled with imitation hooch for Robert, and a new supply of bogus tobacco for Denis. Once again, the horses are spooked by the shots, but fortunately no one is thrown this time. "Take a minute to steady the horses," calls Andy, stating the obvious. Robert is taken out of shot, and the gunmen fire.

The horses are steadied again, Robert is brought back to the set, and his full bottle is replaced with the broken version. "Cue Denis; final line." The cameras roll, and the horsemen ride out of town.

10:35 AM. Scene 42. The fight is about to begin, but Lister realizes too late that the virus has spread to the A/R unit, and their special skills have evaporated.

The 4H are now on foot, and form a line in front of the livery stables. The remaining cast members are brought in, and the crew moves behind the lights. Robert's coat is liberally dusted down with fuller's earth (a light, powdery substance, often used to dirty down clothing and sometimes people) by Howard Burden, and handed back to the actor.

Nearby, Danny is practicing his Riviera Kid dance; a two-second flamenco step which hell do every time his name is mentioned. "They want comedy, we're going to give it to them!" he announces. In front of the stable, Denis is proving that even gunmen can be fans, as he produces his own camera and takes a few photos of Kryten.

11:00 AM. Robert walks out of saloon, followed by the other cast members, and together they confront the 4H. While Andy walks them through the action, Craig practices with his prop knife. For some strange reason, whenever he plays with the knife, the rest of the cast and crew retreat by a few yards.

During the run-through, Chris's clapping dance as he tries to exit the AR game is greeted with gales of laughter from the crew. Everyone knows it's going to look good on camera.

11:10 AM. Ready to record. Simon warns the crew "not to laugh at the end." Smoke is piped in, and the 4H emerge from the building. Robert walks out of the saloon followed by his three companions.

Denis raises his hands over his head and pauses a moment. An electronic effect will be added to the shot, showing lighting flashing from his hands. In doing so, he taps into the AR game, canceling the special skills of his opponents (guess who?).

Chris approaches the horsemen, secure in his abilities as bare-fist fighter extraordinaire. War steps forward to challenge him. Breathing another stream of fire, he rips a length of wood from the smoking hitching post, and begins beating Chris with it. Realizing he's lost his powers, Chris starts a wild dance; clapping his hands together and tapping his feet in a futile attempt to leave the game. Rob and Doug watch the take on a monitor from several yards away. They're both worried that the scene may be playing a bit slow, but hopefully it can be tightened up with additional shots.

12:00 PM. A dispute arises between writers and director. Andy orders a two-shot of Chris and War from the waist up. By eliminating Chris's feet from the shot Doug points out, he's eliminating the comedy. Andy disagrees, not seeing the humor in the dance. "Then why was everyone laughing, then?" Doug asks him. "Because it was

Chris doing a silly dance!" counters Andy who finally agrees to the wide shot. I wonder if he ever got the joke.

1:00 PM. Scene 43. Lister, Cat and Rimmer struggle to remove their A/R helmets. Danny and Craig mime the removal of their AR helmets, which are unseen in their computerized incarnations, but exist back on Starbug. After several run-throughs, Andy, Rob and Doug step in to discuss the funniest way to do it. They finally settle on Danny's hand grabbing the front of Craig's face, which results in some wonderfully contorted expressions from Craig.

1:50 PM. The 4H advance on Chris, who disappears. The illusion is achieved simply by locking the camera off, and having Chris jump out of frame. On the first take, he lunges to the side instead of out of frame, and another take is required.

2:00 PM. While the crew sets up for the next shot, I take the opportunity to grab some lunch. Instead of breaking for lunch today, the caterer's wagon is open for a few hours, and members of the cast and crew sneak off when they're not involved with a scene.

Eating lunch is a fairly surreal experience. Because they're working such a long day, each member of the Laredo Western Club has been told they're entitled to a free meal, and knots of would-be cowboys are scattered around the muddy pasture near the catering truck. I stop to eat lunch with a group of five or six extras whose British accents clash wildly with their western garb. Hearing my American voice, they question me about the authenticity of their little town. It's an understandable question, but a rather stupid one, as I was never actually present during the growth of the American west. The best I can tell them is that I used to live in Arizona when I was a boy, and this is pretty close to the Old Tucson Film Studio I used to visit. That seems to mollify most of them, although one obnoxious club member seems convinced I was around during the San Francisco Gold Rush.

2:45 PM. Scene 48. The four Gunmen fire at Kryten. As he returns fire, his guns turn into doves that fly skyward. The Gunmen die then disappear.

The showdown between Kryten and the 4H. While Robert gets wired up with explosive charges (a process that makes him a bit nervous), the prop people arrive with a cage full of doves. The basic idea is that Kryten has developed a “dove program” to counteract the evil computer virus, and when he draws his guns, they turn into doves which fly into the air.

Meanwhile, one of Peter’s team glues a set of carved dove attachments to Robert’s guns. Although they won’t actually be seen in close-up, the carvings are nicely done.

The final shot of the scene is done first, where the Four Horsemen fall to the ground dead. Andy has the actors removed, and the cameras roll for their fade-away.

Lost scenes: Kryten’s original exit from the A/R game:

Normal speed. Suddenly, the townsfolk are standing on the street, cheering. *KRYTEN climbs up onto his horse, tips his hat and trots out of town, under the sign, ‘You are now entering Consciousness.’*

. . .

3:20 PM. With Robert wired up, it’s time for the first part of the scene. “No explosions this time!” Simon announces. Robert says his line and they cut. Andy puts him into a wide-legged stance, as if Robert is drawing his guns.

One by one, the charges go off. Robert staggers back as if feeling the impact of several bullets, and then pulls out his own guns. Holding them for a second, he allows the weapons to fall to the ground. A small morph will be added to the footage, changing his guns into doves.

“Don’t move a muscle with your feet, Robert!” cautions the director. A pair of doves are brought in and placed in Robert’s hands. “Action!” He pulls them out and lets the birds fly-almost. Instead of taking wing, the doves, whose wings have been clipped by their trainer, promptly float to the ground.

A second take produces the same result. These birds have no intention of flying anywhere today, nor could they if they wanted to. Andy tells Robert to throw them a bit harder; the birds actually have to be seen in flight long enough to put in a morph. After several unsatisfying takes, Andy has to settle for falling, rather than flying birds.

3:40 PM. As Robert bolts from the saloon and down the main street, Wragg's FX men prepare to drop their prop sign on his head. The timing couldn't be more perfect. Even from a distance, Robert's fall looks fantastic, and the crew applauds loudly. Andy is pleased with the take, and Robert goes off to have some minor repair work done on his head.

4:00 PM. An establishing shot of the street. This is the view of Laredo that Lister, Rimmer and Cat will see when they tap into Kryten's dreams. Extras are positioned at various points along the street, and a stagecoach is sent to the far end to await its cue. Andy calls for action, and Gerard Naprous, who's also acting as the episode's stunt coordinator, drives the coach down the street. As it passes the marshal's office, Robert staggers across the street and into the saloon.

Lost scenes: The original entrance of Sheriff Kryten.

A well-dressed WHITE-COLLAR COUPLE are crossing from the other direction. KRYTEN staggers to a halt and, swaying, squints at them to see who they are.

KRYTEN: Evening Ma'am… Jeff.

JEFF: Evening (Ironic), Sheriff.

KRYTEN: Say, Jeff (wipes back of his hand across his mouth)… *you wouldn't happen to have* a couple of nickels going spare, only I got me a bad case of trail throat.

JEFF: You got yourself a bad case of drunken bum sheriff disease, that's what you got.

The COUPLE walk off. KRYTEN stagger toward the saloon. He spots a Wanted poster on the saloon front:

"Wanted- Dead or Dead. The Four Apocalypse Boys: War, Famine, Death and Pestilence. All information to Sheriff Kryten."

KRYTEN looks around sneakily, rips down the poster, scrunches it up and casts it to the ground. He gathers what remains of his dignity, throws open the saloon door and strides in. We follow the srunched-up poster as it blows down the street with the tumble weed.

Suddenly a booted, spurred foot stomps down on it and grinds it into the ground. Backshot: The FOUR HORSEMEN OF THE APOCLYPSE. Three on horseback, the leader holding his horse, move off down the street towards the saloon.

...

4:45 PM. Craig, Chris and Danny are put on horseback for their ride into town. Although Chris seems awfully nervous about the idea, and Craig is cautiously enjoying it, Danny is having a ball. He's spent a good part of his of-camera time riding, although the fact that his horse is named Pee Wee has led to several tasteless comments throughout the day.

"We are rapidly losing the light!" announces John Pomphrey, who has been keeping one eye skyward for most of the day. As if realizing the impact of his words, the crew seems to pick up their pace. They return to the saloon, where Death spits a stream of acidic tobacco on Kryten's boot. Peter Wragg is called in, and he sprinkles a tiny quantity of TCC, a terribly caustic liquid at Robert's feet. The compound is so hazardous it can only be used out of doors, and one crew members makes a silly crack about Peter "dropping acid." Several takes are needed to get a shot that looks convincing. [Ironically, the shot is cut from the final version of 'Gunmen.']

4:55 PM. Once again, John Pomphrey, the lighting prophet of doom announces the growing lack of natural illumination. With less than 15 minutes of usable light remaining, Craig, Chris and Danny and their respective horses are lined up in front of the stables. The extras are called down to that end of the street. Doreen, an elderly extra, walks carefully across the street. A few seconds later, the three would-be cowboys ride in. Leaving their horses in front of the saloon, they enter the building. Those interior scenes will be shot in the studio on Thursday.

5:05 PM. Andy wants to get one more shot of the actors entering the saloon. As they emerge into the fading sunlight, Danny looks into the camera and announces, "There's no one there!" That bit is followed by a quick shot of Kryten running out of the saloon and down the street.

5:10 PM. The last setup of the day is a special shot of all four cast members riding into town on horseback. Although the scene doesn't actually take place in 'Gunmen,' Rob and Doug want the shot for the opening credit sequence. Rocket is lifted into the air on his crane (a piece of equipment that Rob and Doug initially resisted for this episode, I later find out) and Tony one of the other cameramen gets into position for a low shot looking up at the group as they ride past.

"People are going to say, 'Where did they get the money for that location?'" John Pomphrey says with satisfaction, looking at the monitor. After a second take, Andy, Rob and Doug get a shot they're happy with and Simon announces, "That's a wrap!" Just in time too, as the sun dips down over the street of Laredo. The cast and crew are happy and excited, after what may be the most successful filming day of Red Dwarf VI.

The Four Horsemen

Denis Lill (Death)

How did you wind up doing this story?

Dennis Lill: This happened as a result of The 10%ers. We had a big press release that Rob and Doug were at. I asked them how Red Dwarf was going and they said, 'Oh, we're having a lot of fun; we're doing a Western-' I grabbed them by the collars and said, 'I'd kill to do a Western!' So that's how it came about.

Is this the first time you've done a Western?

Lill: Yes. Like most English actors, I've fantasized about it for some time. Liam Neeson is a great mate of mine, and we used to go and see all the Westerns together- mainly the Sergio Leone/Clint Eastwood ones and fantasize about being in a western. We used to fill ourselves with beer and watch them over and over again.

Had you followed *Red Dwarf* up until now?

Lill: I've only caught the last two episodes, but I'm absolutely hooked on it now! My only complaint is the episodes aren't long enough. They seem to cram a hell of a lot into them.

What was the most fun about doing this episode?

Lill: Oh, everything about it: getting on the gear, the guns, the horses, the town; the whole bit has been brilliant.

You seem to be pretty adept at riding a horse.

Lill: In a sense, I've been training for this day for my entire life. I was born and brought up in New Zealand, and I've always kept my riding up, because in this profession, one is required to ride from time to time. These horses are a bit spooky today. When somebody fires a .45 close to your ear, you're bound to react in some way or other.

You've had some brushes with SF before, including a Doctor Who story about a million year ago.

Lill: That's right, I did one with Tom Baker, and another one a few years later with Peter Davison. That was another riding job; the director just offered me a job in Dorset, living in a hotel, and riding a horse for a week.

Dinny Powell (Famine)

Do you consider yourself an actor or a stuntman?

Dinny Powell: I'm a combination of both. I do a lot of car stuff now, but I've also got my own horses, so Gerard called and asked me to play the part of Famine and to ride a horse. He knew there would be guns going off, and we might have a little problem. The horses are trained for the guns, but they're unpredictable when it comes to compressed air going off. For some unknown reason, it always spooks them, so Gerard said he'd better get me down here just in case. I've been working close to the actors, because the other stunt guy had to do the flames, so his hands were already occupied. I just kept the others moving.

Was this supposed to be a speaking part?

Powell: Just somebody to be on the horse. When Gerard called and said, "Okay, put your old stuff on; you might take a tumble!" I said okay, I'd be ready for it.

Is this padding you're wearing now?

Powell: Yeah, it's to make me look like Famine. I've got so much padding on me that I can hardly move. If I had fallen off the horse, I'd have bounced!

I'll bet Robert wished he had been wearing it when he got thrown this morning.

Powell: The horse spun on him, and I couldn't grab its head quickly enough as it turned. Then of course, my horse reared up, so there's a time when everyone takes care of themselves, but it behaved very well. It's never gunshots because they get used to that, but they don't get used to compressed air!

Robert Inch (War)

How does one train as a fire-eater?

Robert Inch: Most of it comes down to yourself, really. You get shown what to do, and then you practice with water and so forth. After that, it's seeing how far you can go with it.

But it still remains dangerous.

Inch: Most definitely. Especially outside, and on horseback.

How did you do the stunt today?

Inch: That was paraffin which is what I would normally use. I rehearsed the stunt at home a couple of times, but it was the first time I'd ever done it.

Had you followed *Red Dwarf* before?

Inch: Oh yeah, I love the program. I wasn't sure what I was going to be doing, until I found out I was going to be one of the Four Gunmen of the Apocalypse. It was going to be a western as well, which was great.

Jeremy Peters (Pestilence)

How did you get the part of Pestilence?

Jeremy Peters: My agent got a call and the casting director had obviously seen my photo. I think that's how they picked me, and the fact that I ride, so that probably helped. They said I'd be playing Pestilence, one of the Four Horsemen. Those are sort of the roles I get: quirky characters like Blind Pew in Treasure Island, Dillinger; those kind of characters.

How long did your Pestilence makeup take to apply?

Peters: We started at 6:30 this morning and finished at 7:45. It was really just putting on the little bits of latex and then gelatin.

Did you enjoy playing a villainous cowboy?

Peters: I've played a cowboy before, in a play, deconstructing the American myth of cowboys from the viewpoint of a western enthusiast. This guy is taken back to America in this dream world, where he realizes his view of the west is totally different from the reality. That was my last taste of playing a cowboy, being a little boy and dressing up!

...

Before I leave, I ask Steve Bradshaw if I can take the Wanted poster that's been tacked on the saloon. Originally, there was a large stack of spare posters inside the saloon, just in case something should happen to the original, but throughout the day, Laredo club members have been removing them to be autographed by the cast. The poster outside is the last one left, but Steve tells me it will just be removed and thrown away now that filming is over. I carefully take it down and take it with me. The poster will go to a Red Dwarf convention in a few weeks where it will raise money in the charity auction. One fan will be soon have a rare memento of Red Dwarf VI.

Thursday, March 11. Pre-VT Day: 'Gunmen of the Apocalypse.'

10:00 AM. After Tuesday's location filming, today's studio recording is a bit of an anti-climax, although there's lots of work to be done. The centerpiece of the day will be the saloon fight, which will see Lister using his knife-throwing skills, the Riviera Kid shooting his opponents' bullets out of the air, and a fist fight between Rimmer and a trio of toughs. Oh, and Liz Hickling returns as a simulant, along with her commander, Denis (Death) Lill.

On the far side of Stage G, Mel Bibby's team have built an impressive-looking saloon set, which will be the center for most of today's action. Several extras dressed in western clothing are already hanging around the set, waiting for their first scene. A gorgeous blonde woman in a red dress and feathers (on the dress, that is) is leaning against the bar. Although most of the people are new, I recognize Gerard the stunt coordinator, who has brought along a few of his men for the fight sequences.

A tall actor dressed in black walks onto the set and is seated at a table where several extras are playing cards. This is Jimmy the town bully, who will be getting his just deserts before the end of the day. Around the table, Howard's wardrobe people bustle back and forth, checking costumes.

10:10 AM. Robert enters, in makeup and his western clothing from Tuesday. Andy brings him through the saloon doors and walks him through today's first scene, in which Kryten meets Jimmy. A large woman in a tacky dress steps behind the bar and starts familiarizing herself with the props. This is Imogen Bain, who will be playing Lola the bartender.

10:15 AM. Run-through. Kryten staggers in, and is tripped by Jimmy. One of the cowboys pokes his head in the door to announce the arrival of the Apocalypse Boys. The extras duck behind their tables and chairs, while Robert grabs a bottle, takes a swig, and staggers out the door.

After the scene, chairs are repositioned on small pieces of red tape that have lain down to mark positions. Simon tells Robert the scene has been readjusted, and explains the changes to him.

10:30 AM. Another run-through. Everyone ducks for cover as Jimmy challenges the drunken sheriff with the funny head. During a free moment, Andria's assistant Lois Burwell steps in to adjust Kryten's neck.

11:00 AM. Gerard and his stunt man step outside Stage G to practice their fight sequence with Chris. The moves are fairly simple, but the scene will be played for laughs and should look quite good. Chris seems very enthusiastic, which isn't surprising. During his last bar brawl in 'Backwards,' Rimmer didn't do much more than hide. This time, he gets to have a little fun.

10:05 AM. I sit down next to Paul McGuiness, who is helping Peter on set today. Tomorrow, he'll be back in the BBC's West Acton workshop, working on the Polyhawk for next week's episode. He doesn't have much lead time. The script was delivered to the department heads during the OB filming Tuesday afternoon, and the front page had a note reading "Not for the eyes of cast." Talk about waving a red flag in front of a bull.

At any rate, Paul tells me he may be playing the GELF leader who carries the Polyhawk around for part of the episode. This would make his job easier, because he could then design the creature as a puppet around his own arm. It's too early to tell, although Paul did attend yesterday's production meeting where he was told about his possible role.

11:15 AM. Scene 35. Lister comes to Kryten's rescue, and with some fancy knife throwing, pins Jimmy down. Steve Devereaux, the actor playing Jimmy is filmed holding his pistol out and then bolstering it. The shot will be played backwards making it look as though the actor's arm has been pinned to a wall. The scene requires numerous takes before Andy gets a shot he likes.

11:45 AM. Andy asks the FX boys if they have a prop chair that can be used for Chris's fight scene this afternoon. Obviously this causes a great deal of laughter, as though the boys have a ready supply of breakaway chairs they carry around with them.

I sit down in one of the chairs in the mid-section, where Robert and Chris are waiting to be called. Robert is quietly conserving his energy as he often does between takes, while Chris is silently mouthing lines from his next scene. Danny walks up, in his Riviera Kid costume. He has a terrible pun he wants to put in today's script, and bets his fellow cast members it will get in. Andy walks over to talk with the actors, particularly Craig who has a difficult knife-throwing sequence today.

12:15PM. The boys are called in for their next scene, where Rimmer vomits into the hat of Bearstrangler McGee. The erstwhile Mr. McGee is played by a small mountain named Stephen Marcus, who looks like he could break Chris in half without breaking a sweat. The simple act of standing up results in plenty of laughs, and he hasn't even said a word yet.

Standing off to one side of the set, Craig is standing with a group of stagehands and electricians. One of the sparks tells him that he and Danny should do a remake of Butch Cassidy, called Butch

Coconut and the Sunburn Kid. The joke sounds a bit racist to me, but Craig seems to get a laugh from it.

12:45 PM. Ready to record. Rimmer's vomit scene goes, excuse the expression, very well. It's certainly one of the big laughs of the saloon sequence.

Producer Justin Judd walks over to Paul, and asks him if he's ready to be a GELF. "Do you have any idea what this entails in terms of makeup?" It's three hours in the chair, which doesn't sound like a lot of fun. Justin also asks the potential GELF how tall he is. Obviously there's some sort of height requirement in being a genetically engineered life form.

1:05 PM. Simon calls for hubbub in the bar, which suddenly stops when the three Dwarfers enter. The take goes okay, but Andy decides to do one more.

1:15 PM. Simon asks Lola to spit a cork into Rimmer's face. To Chris's discomfort, this has to be done several times until they get it right. By the time lunch rolls around, he's been "corked" more than half a dozen times.

2:30 PM. The cast and crew start trickling back in from lunch. Carl the armorer dispenses weapons to the actors on their way to makeup. Shooting resumes with Kryten meeting his former companions, and ends with a bottle jerked out of his hand. That's when it starts to get complicated.

3:25 PM. Scene 35. Jimmy pulls the whiskey bottle out of Kryten's hand with a bullwhip. A breakaway whip has been built, with a bottle attached to one end, so it will appear that one of Lister's knives has cut the whip in half. A shot of the knife stuck in the wall be added as a separate element.

In order to show the other knives pinning Jimmy's arms to the saloon wall, the shot actually has to be recorded and played backwards. The actor stands against the wall with a knife already affixed to his sleeve. The other end is attached to a line of monofilament. Paul McGuiness stands on a chair a few feet away, and pulls the knife out of the wall. A simple solution perhaps, but the effect has to be repeated several times to look convincing. The same camera trick is then used for a shot of an apple flying into Jimmy's mouth. It's a very time-consuming effect.

4:45 PM. Craig is called back to the set for the other half of the shot, where Lister (AKA Brett Riverboat) throws his knives at Jimmy. Robert is brought in, complaining loudly about his proximity to Craig's knives.

The scene should be relatively easy to shoot, but when Craig tries to impale an apple an apple with his knife and flip it at Jimmy, the apple sticks to the blade and refuses to move. Much to the crew's amusement, it takes several tries before Craig manages to dislodge the apple.

5:05 PM. "Everyone on the set please!" With a thunder of cowboy boots and the clang of several sets of spurs, the extras take their place in the saloon. The next segment has Jimmy dangling a bottle from his whip in front of Kryten. The scene is quite effective, thanks to Robert's acting ability.

5:15 PM. The whip breaks and Kryten grabs the bottle, with part of the whip still coiled around it.

5:30 PM. Denis Lill arrives, dressed as the simulant captain. He's wearing a black leather outfit trimmed in silver, and looks like he's just parked his Harley outside. His makeup consists of a waxy foundation and a set of double eyebrows. He's still wearing his own mustache, which was rumored to come off after Tuesday, but apparently Denis resisted the pressure to remove it. A few minutes later, Liz Hickling joins him, dressed as the other simulant Since 'Gunmen' takes place before 'Rimmerworld,' which was recorded last week, she looks considerably less damaged for today's recording.

5:40 PM. Scene 35. Cat next demonstrates his prowess as a gunfighter. Time for the Riviera Kid to show his stuff. Simon announces that a gun will be fired in this scene, where the Kid draws his pistols against two of Jimmy's thugs. The stunt men draw their weapons at blinding speed and fire, but something seems to have gone wrong. Something- part of a blank charge perhaps- hits Danny, who complains, "I've got some kind of shit on my face!" A hasty examination shows the actor unharmed, but he's still shaken up.

For the second part of the sequence, Danny shoots his own guns. An electronic effect will be added, as if the gunmen's' bullets have just been shot out of the air.

6:00 PM. "During this next bit, we all stay on the floor, chaps," Simon tells the extras. They stay crouched on the floor, while Robert exits the saloon.

6:10 PM. Simon asks the crew to postpone their dinner break, "just until after the fight scene." There are some groans from crew members who know the scene won't be finished in the 15-20 minutes promised.

6:15 PM. Chris, Gerard and several stunt men run through Rimmer/Dangerous Dan's big fight scene. It goes very well, with Chris throwing cowboys into the air, over the bar and into the wall. The fight is restaged three times. Andy thinks the second take is best, but will probably cut it together with other takes. With that scene finished, it's time for dinner.

7:40 PM. With less then three hours left, there are a few saloon shots left to finish, as well as the simulant battle scenes. First, it's time to finish in the saloon. The last scene has the boys trying to sober up Kryten by spooning dried coffee (really powdered chocolate) into his mechanoid mouth.

8:05 PM. Ready to record. Gill steps in to replace Danny's tie which has fallen off during the run-through. The first take looks good, but Andy decides to do one more for safety. Meanwhile, vision supervisor Mike Spencer plays with the picture, giving it a sepia tone. Watching the monitor, the scene looks like a vintage picture postcard.

8:15 PM. With the last saloon scene finished, the cast comes over to watch the playback on the monitor. "What a lovely posse we make," jokes Robert, "until I take my mask off; then you've got that ugly git, Robert Llewellyn."

"Then you can be a posse by yourself," Craig retorts.

Carl the armourer walks around the set, collecting weapons, and the cowboy extras are released. While the cast go off to change costumes, lights go on in the mid-section, and the crew moves in to set up.

8:30 PM. Denis wanders back in, and Liz walks up, putting one arm around him. "Don't we look great together?" she laughs. "Your eyebrows look great," she tells Denis. "I wish mine would go up like that!" Denis's response: "You should have been a boy."

The simulant ship is actually Rimmer's escape pod from last week, partially redressed, and with an additional front console. With careful lighting, most viewers probably won't notice, especially since this episode will be aired first.

8:45 PM. Craig returns to the set, dressed in his Lister costume. He's carrying his boots in one hand. Behind him, Robert walks in, minus his plastic chest plate.

Andria walks up to her assistant Annie McEwan, who normally handles Danny's makeup, and hands her a small plastic tube containing a fake eyeball. "This has to be put on Danny's chin," she says. "Don't ask any questions."

9:00 PM. 1 sit down with Robert, Rocket and one of the other cameramen, who are sitting around the table in the mid-section. Chris walks in, dressed in his blue hard light uniform. Robert asks him to do his impression of Simon, which is letter-perfect. Chris has crept up behind Craig and Danny several times over the last few weeks, and in his best Simon voice, yelled, "Quiet on the set please!" Both Craig and Danny shut up instantly before realizing they've just been had. Now all four cast members have their own Simon impressions, although Chris's version is by far the best.

Craig walks in, with a fake eyeball stuck to his chin. He's ready for the final scene of the night where Lister and the Cat try to fool the simulants by pretending to be aliens. "Danny, don't you have yours on yet?" Annie walks over and starts applying Danny's third eye.

Meanwhile, the simulant scenes are being shot. Bathed in an eerie blue light the set looks completely different from the escape pod of last week. Rob and Doug arrive on the set and watch the scene on a monitor. They smile, watching Liz and Denis playing the simulants. I tell Rob that Denis looks like one of the munchkins from The Wizard of Oz, with the eyebrows and mustache. Rob smiles. "I thought he looked like Groucho Marx!"

9:15 PM. Scene 24. The two simulants realize they are goners. The one last sting in their tail is to hack into Starbug's Navicomp and transmit the Armageddon virus.

The simulant ship begins to explode. Sparks fly all over the set, with one big explosion at the end. Unfortunately, the take doesn't look entirely convincing, and the FX crew has to reset all the charges.

9:35 PM. Denis and Liz return to the ship for another take. This one looks even better, ending with a wonderful close-up on Denis.

9:45 PM. The last scene of the day. Craig and Danny are seated in the mid-section, with fake eyeballs pasted to their chins. The camera is turned upside down so the bottom of their heads is on top. Robert stands behind them, holding a fake camera over them, as though he is transmitting the image back to the simulant ship. That's followed by Denis materializing on Starbug.

The scene proves to be too complex to finish tonight. Denis will have to be brought back on Saturday for an extra day of recording. Simon calls a wrap, and another long day is over.

Saturday, March 13. Audience Recording Day: 'Gunmen of the Apocalypse'

2:00 PM. A new addition has been added to the ops set. The teleport pad from last week's episode has been re-dressed, with the words "A-R Unit" painted on it, and a metal railing that encloses three sides.

The FX team has created a set of Artificial Reality helmets for the cast, while costume was responsible for the accompanying boot, gloves and groinal attachments.

Craig removes his blue sunglasses- a trademark of Saturday rehearsals- and pulls on his helmet. It's made to fit around the head, with a fold-down visor covered with blinking lights.

3:00 PM. Scene 4. *Kryten dressed in artificial reality gear prepares to enter Lister's fantasy world.* Robert types into a computer keyboard in front of a monitor labeled "Artificial Reality Console." The title Gumshoe appears, followed by a selection of characters from the AR game. Robert settles on Sammy the Squib. These scenes will recorded tonight, and cut together with the black and white footage shot last week. Another prop that has to be moved in and out of ops is the medical bed where Kryten will be placed after contracting the computer virus.

3:30 PM Stagger-through. Tonight's recording should be relatively easy. A large chunk has been pre-recorded over the last few weeks, so most of remaining scenes take place in the cockpit. The major exception is the Vindalooian Ambassador sequence, which has to be re-shot.

6:30 PM. Saturday's dinner is always my favorite part of the week. It's not because the food in the Shepperton canteen is any good (it certainly isn't!); it's because of the company. Every Saturday night, I join Ron Green, Jackie one of his crew, John Pomphrey, his associate Dai Thomas who works in the lighting van, and Jeff Jeffrey. At least two people bring a really nice bottle of wine with them, making dinner an enjoyable, relaxing break at the end of the week.

Tonight, I bring in my own bottle, as a small way of saying thanks. This particular group of people have been friendly to me since the first week of filming, often taking the time to explain how a shot is being lit, or what sort of technical problems have to be met that day. My understanding of the recording process has gone up by a thousand percent thanks to their help.

Before the end of dinner, Sheelagh arrives to join us for tonight's recording. The crew invites her to join them for a glass of wine, and she's able to meet the people I've been working with for the last several weeks.

7:30 PM. Even with a relatively small number of scenes, tonight's recording is not without its flubs and fluffs. Whether it's because of a lack of recording time, or

because there are less scenes to shoot, the cast seems to be making a large number of gaffes. To the audience's delight, most of them are quite funny.

It starts with Craig and Robert emerging from the AR game. When Craig turns around, he walks right into the metal railing, which collides with a sensitive area of his anatomy.

Then we move into the cockpit, where Rimmer announces, "At last, we have silent running!" He leans over the Cat, who's piloting Starbug, and tells him, "Long range scanners are down. The only early warning we've got is you- stay alert!" Danny's only line is "Okay Bud, I'll keep my nose peeled!" but instead, he completely misses his cue. There's a long pause, and Chris slaps Danny in the arm. The audience howls with laughter, especially in light of Chris's setup line.

After that, it's Chris's turn. He meets Craig who's just returned from the AR game, and starts lecturing him about his liaison with an under-age ball girl in the Wimbledon AR game. Chris's line should be, "Lister, she's a computer sprite, a load of pixels, but somehow it comes out, "Lister, she's a computer pa...pussy!" That one breaks up the crew as well.

And finally, there's poor Robert, who just can't get around his cockpit speech, volunteering to contract the simulant computer virus. In an early take, he tells Rimmer, "Sir, the only thing I can suggest is that I contract the virus myself, analyze its structure, and attempt to...stop there before I go any further into a big pile of poo!" In another take, he gets a little further, saying, "analyze its structure and attempt to create a software antidote before it wipes out my core program- do I have your permission to...poo myself sir?" It's even funnier, because he stays in character.

Scene 16. O/S simulants as they look into their monitor. A strange alien life form appears on screen. It is Lister, disguised as a creature with cheap props (anything not to look like a humanoid). He claims to be Tarka Dall, an Ambassador of the Vindalooian Empire. Cal appears on the monitor similarly "doctored. "

Rounding out the evening is the re-shoot of Thursday's scenes, where Lister and Cat impersonate an alien crew, with the aid of a skillfully placed eyeball or two. Tonight, the sequence has been re-staged, so instead of putting the two characters in chairs, they're lying across a table with Robert standing over them with a camera. Obviously this gives him a chance to tell Craig, "As long as you're down there..."

The biggest problems are the eyeballs. When Craig and Danny sit up, they're supposed to remove the eyes from their chins and hand them back to Robert, who pops them back into his own sockets. Easy, right? In one take, Robert drops an eye which rolls away. The blinded Kryten stays in character, popping in the remaining orb.

Another attempt results in Danny sitting up, and his eyeball rolling down his front. Meanwhile, Denis stays in character as the simulant captain, watching these events without smiling. He may be the only one in the studio who does.

In due course, the night's recording is over. Both cast and crew are very excited about Gunmen, and it looks like it will be the high point of season six. Although it's still too early to tell, I think they may be right.

Thursday, March 18. Pre-VT Day: 'Polymorph II: Emohawk.'

10:00 AM. Stage G is already a beehive of activity. The mid-section set is piled high with storage containers and crates. Wires and cables hang from the ceiling, as well as ducting, machine parts, loose springs, etc. In this week's episode, Starbug is in bad shape after crash landing on a swampy planet, hence the total disarray.

Next door in the galley, Mel and Steve are installing a section of Plexiglas countertop, which has a large circular hole cut out of its center. A large can of baked beans marked "Beinz" is nearby.

Liz the animal trainer comes in, and Rina starts going over today's scenes with her. Liz has brought an entire menagerie with her, including a frog, a chicken, a rabbit and a chinchilla; all waiting to make their Red Dwarf debut.

On the far side of the stage, the saloon from 'Gunmen' has been replaced by the interior of a primitive hut, which will double as the GELF chieftain's hut and Lister's honeymoon suite. The set has mock stone walls, an arched wooden ceiling, and several furs and barrels scattered around. A dead rabbit hangs over the entrance, with another against the wall, along with various primitive artifacts. A deteriorating human skulls rests against a window.

A few feet away, the FX crew assemble their gear for the day. They've got a lot to do in this episode, including smoke, burning torches, explosive charges, and several versions of the title creature. A large bucket holds four puppet Emohawks, as the critter is now being called, and a fleshy sucker on a long stick, which will be used for close-ups.

10:15 AM. Danny arrives, in costume and makeup. He is wearing the same black PVC trousers and boots, with a multi-colored vest and striped jacket. Andy runs him through the first scene, in which Cat looks into a can of beans and discovers the Emohawk.

While we're watching the rehearsal, Jeff Jeffrey tells me the script for episode six won't be ready until Monday, which is very late. He gives me a quick synopsis of the story, but says it doesn't have a resolution yet. "We don't know if the next series will be called Red Dwarf or Green Bug," he comments.

10:20 AM. Scene 30. Cat follows the Emohawk's scent trail back into the galley. Ready to record the first scene. Danny picks up the baked bean can and calls to the others that he's found the creature.

After the shot, Steve and James get the baked beans ready. It's a dirty job, but someone's got to do it. Danny stands off camera, waiting to go back on. Ron Green walks up. "Nice jacket," he says, admiring Danny's costume.

"That's right up the street," is the response. "And that's Quality Street, isn't it?"

10:30 AM. Scene 31. The Emohawk shoots out of the can of beans. Cat is suckered.

Paul the cameraman stands on a stool, with his camera looking down into the can of beans. Wanting a better shot, he steps on top of the counter, looking straight down. Meanwhile, Paul McGuiness is underneath, manipulating the beans through a false bottom, as though something is inside the can. As Danny reacts to what he sees, the beans begin to churn violently.

Paul steps out from beneath the counter, and removes the glove which had been connected to the bottom of the can. James returns with one of the Emohawk puppets, which he places on Danny's hand. Never missing an opportunity, Danny entertains himself by doing an impromptu puppet show. "This would be great for Saturday morning!" he announces.

Paul places a plastic bag over his upper body, while James puts a new can over the round hole cut into the counter. Paul slides the puppet over his hand and slides under the counter. On cue, he'll stick an Emohawk-covered hand up through the bottom of the can.

11:00 AM. Ready to record. Danny picks up can, and the Emohawk erupts from it in a shower of baked beans. The take looks convincing, but Andy wants another one. Paul removes the puppet, the area is cleaned up, and the can of beans replaced for another take.

11:15 AM. "Can we bring in the sucker, please?" asks Andy. Paul steps out, and Danny is brought back in to rehearse the scene of the Emohawk's sucker hitting him in the forehead. John Pomphrey puts a red gel in one of the front lights, and Danny quips, "It's the old red wash again!" He crosses his eyes and opens his mouth, remembering a similar scene in 'Polymorph' a few seasons ago.

There are several takes, as the sucker keeps missing Danny's forehead, hitting him in the eye, a cheek; anywhere but where it's supposed to be. "That's show biz!" comments Danny, after being hit in the eye with a sucker for the umpteenth time. James and Nick move in behind the counter to catch him as he falls.

11:25 AM. Scene 33. Paper airplane hits Rimmer's desk. He scrunches it up and throws it in the bin.

"Chris in the cockpit please!" Danny returns to makeup where he'll be changed into Duane Dibbly, and Chris seats himself in the cockpit. For this scene, the Emohawk transforms itself into a paper plane and flies into the cockpit. Rimmer crumbles it up and throws it away. On the first take, the plane hits Chris in the head, but take number two is fine.

11:45 AM. Scene 36. The microphone becomes the Emohawk. Rimmer is suckered.

Andy calls for "William Tell" McGuiness, who arrives, pole-mounted sucker in hand. He rehearses hitting Chris in the forehead with it; more successfully than with Danny.

12:00 PM. Danny returns to the set, still dressed in Cat's clothes, but with Duane Dibbly's buck teeth and wig. In the next scene, Duane walks out of the galley, transformed into his nerdish alter-ego. It's going to be a difficult scene to get in one take because of all the camera movement.

"On to Duane in the kitchen!" announces Simon. Chris gets a break before returning to makeup for his Ace wig, and Danny steps into the galley where several cabinets have been filled with noisy pots and pans.

12:45 PM. Scene 34. Cat becomes Duane Dibbly.

This scene is going to be a real crowd-pleaser, as a transformed Duane emerges slowly from below the counter, revealing first the top of his head, then his eyes, his teeth and the rest of his face. He fumbles around for a mirror, banging his head on a cabinet. Opening it, he's deluged with pots and pans which crash loudly all around him. Grabbing one pot, he sees himself in the mirrored surface and utters those immortal words, "Duane Dibbly? DUANE DIBBLY? AAAAAGGHH!" Only a few takes are needed to finish the scene, and Simon calls for a lunch break.

2:15 PM. The cast assembles in the engine room set. Chris is dressed in his blue Rimmer uniform, while Danny has changed into the now-familiar Duane Dibbly outfit and anorak. Coming back from lunch, he was still jubilant from the morning's shoot. Danny had pushed for a slow reveal of Duane, as he came up from the counter, but Andy, who wasn't really familiar with the character, wanted to shoot it faster. In the end, Danny managed to get what he wanted, and he's looking forward to seeing how the scene plays in front of the live audience on Saturday.

Meanwhile, two of the GELFs arrive for makeup. The GELF bride is Steve Wickham, an old friend of mine, who's worked on the Panopticon Doctor Who conventions here in the UK for years. He seems surprised to see me in Shepperton Studios of all places, until I explain to him I'm writing a book about the series.

The GELF chief is played by a tall black actor named Ainsley Harriott. He's cheerful, friendly and looking forward to appearing in Red Dwarf, albeit under a ton of fake GELF fur. Ainsley is also an expert chef, which probably pays a lot more than his acting work.

Steve and Ainsley go to makeup, where over the next two hours they'll be transformed into GELFs. It's a two hour process, involving a prosthetic mask, furry body suit, and a molded chest plate and buttocks that were sculpted by Paul McGuiness. It's a thoroughly unpleasant-looking outfit, which should look great on camera.

In the ops room, Jeff starts setting up for tonight's second unit filming. While the first unit goes out to the nearby back lot, the second unit will remain in the studio, shooting all the scenes involving animals, transformations, etc. The camera has to be locked off while objects are replaced; a long and tedious process. By shooting these FX simultaneously, the crew can get twice as much work done tonight.

2:30 PM. Scene 39. Kryten and Lister arrive just as Rimmer/Ace fails to break Cat/Duane 's neck. They go to the ops room in search of the Emohawk.

The boys make their way through the engine room, shooting at anything that moves (and sometimes, what doesn't move). The scene has to be re-shot several times, and with each take, Peter's team has to reset the charges.

Between takes, the other cast members make fun of Danny's Duane persona. The best gag is Duane's World, a catch-phrase that will be repeated throughout the week.

Dressed in his stifling costume, Danny is trying to stay calm and not exert himself too much. He tells me that after this morning's scenes, he was soaked through with perspiration.

Paul McGuiness (Visual FX)

You built the Emohawk?

McGuinness: The closest I got to a description was that it was supposed to be another polymorph, a cross between a slavering dog and peeled brains. It was not going to have wings that looked like it worked. It could just change into whatever it wanted to, so it had jokey feathers, which was as close as it would get to wings.

How long did it take to sculpt up?

McGuinness: A day and a half to sculpt and half a day to mold it, and then I cast four different ones. There's a puppet version, which is the one you see the most of, and a shorter one with its eyes closed. The one that comes out of the beans has all its eyes closed, which you probably never notice; and one to go on Lister's head as a hat, which was cast over Craig's head cast so that it would sit neatly on his head. Then there's a complete one, which was originally for the scene where Danny was prodding around in the undergrowth with a stick and realizes the stick is it. That was the general stunt version. The complete one had an armature inside it so you could open and close its mouth, and you could bend its neck or body into any position you wanted.

The thing is, I think Andy was expecting it to have some animatronic movement; he wanted it to roll its eyes, blink and things like that. Andy worked on Spitting Image, so he's used to seeing things that have lots of facial movements in them. It probably didn't occur to him that we only had a limited amount of time to build them, and there's no way we could have gotten any of that in. If I had a couple of weeks, I could have made its eyes blink, but not in four days.

The sucker was very straightforward; it's a very rough sculpt on a steel pole, with a sculpted end which you probably wouldn't see either, because there weren't any straight on-shots of it. Originally, I did make another sucker to come out of its mouth which they never shot, which was literally a collapsible version of the sucker on a steel rod.

You did all the puppeteering yourself?

McGuinness: It was a bit awkward because I had to strain was really to get around a chair and a fat belly, which was the costume the chap was wearing. It was also difficult to know what was going on. I stole the little monitor from the psi-scan and used it to see what was going on, but it was still very difficult to see.

What kind of work did you do on the GELFS?

McGuinness: Howard Burden and I discussed them over lunch the day before I did them. They were supposed to be very fat with pendulous breasts, and warty, which was more or less how they were described in the script. They were very quick to do; it only took a few hours to sculpt, because the larger the thing is, the easier it is to sculpt I find. When it gets smaller, the more detail you have to put in. With something that's very big, you can get away with putting in very rough detail and not have to put in all those fine wrinkles. It only took a few hours to sculpt the bellies and bums, and they were generally big, spotty lumpy things with rolls of flesh and pierced nipples and stuff like that.

Were you relieved you didn't have to play one after all?

McGuinness: It was a relief, because I didn't fancy having to sit in the makeup chair for two or three hours and warts stuck all over my head. It would have been easier to do the puppeteering than being inside it, especially the one shot where during the shot, I had to quickly pull my arm out and slip it in the dummy Emohawk, as the GELF gets up and leaves the room. I was puppeteering during a bit of dialogue between Craig and Kryten, so I had to take my arm out and stick the other one under his arm and get out of the shot. I suppose it would have been easier to have been in, carrying on puppeteering it all the way out of the shot. It's like anything else: there are pluses and minuses.

...

Lost scenes: The airlock scene with Duane and Ace, was trimmed considerably in the final episode.

RIMMER/ACE: Just relax, old chum. Just sending you on ahead.

CAT/DUANE: I'm the scout party?

RIMMER/ACE: Sort of.

CAT/DUANE: Can I ask you a question?

RIMMER/ACE: Fire away, Mr. D.

CAT/DUANE: Do you think it's wrong for a thirty-two year-old man to... have his own yo-yo?

RIMMER/ACE: No, old friend, that's not wrong. It's totally normal.

CAT/DUANE: And do you think it would be wrong for that same man to sometime want to play round in his polyester balaclava and play with that yo-yo? Practicing some snazzy moves in order to attract women.

RIMMER/ACE releases CAT/DUANE.

RIMMER/ACE: I can't do it, damn it. It's be like garroting Bambi.

...

2:55 PM. The sequence is finally finished, by the fourth or fifth take.

3:05 PM. Scene 41. One of Cat's thermoses turn into the Emohawk. It then turns into a grenade. Rimmer/Ace dives on grenade, producing the Emohawk from underneath him. Lister freezes the Emohawk.

The actual shot of Duane's thermos turning into the Emohawk will be accomplished with another electronic morph. Danny pretends to grapple with the creature, which then turns into a grenade. He then gets ready to throw the grenade away, even though Duane throws like a girl.

3:30 PM. Between scenes, Danny sits down next to Robert in the bleachers, both still in costume. They start discussing what a show called Duane's World would be like; the most naff characters of the week, being interviewed by Duane in a completely tacky set.

4:00 PM. The cast rehearse the scene where Ace throws himself on the grenade. The explosion will be added in post-production, making the sight of Chris spreading himself full-length on the floor a bit silly.

4:10 PM. The grenade turns back into the Emohawk, and Lister freezes it. Rob and Doug worry that the scene doesn't look very realistic. When the puppet hits the floor, it bounces, and when Craig puts his foot on it, it bends.

4:45 PM. Scene 41. Cat/Duane accidentally freezes his companions. The scene will be played over the episode's closing credits. Danny thinks the bit turned out very well. "That one's sealed with a kiss," he says after it's finished. "I'll be banking that one with my Visa card!" Some members of the crew don't agree. There have been several drafts of the script, and the ending has changed each time. My own impression is that Rob and Doug weren't sure how to end this episode, but with time running out, an ending was needed. I guess we'll never know.

Lost scenes: The original ending for 'Emohawk.'

RIMMER/ACE: Is it possible I could stay like this for another twenty-four hours, before I have to return as that ghastly maggot?

*KRYTEN: I don't see why not. What about you, Cat, do you want to stay as Dua*ne?

CAT/DUANE: Suck my thermos!

(Run credits)

...

5:00 PM. The second unit is now set up for tonight's filming. A table to one side of the set is covered with recording equipment, a control unit and monitor. They'll start working as a separate unit in about 15 minutes. Meanwhile, a section of floor has been removed in the ops room and replaced with a tile containing a gaping hole. The boys find the hole, and decide the Emohawk has lasered it's way down to the engine room.

5:15 PM. The crew splits into two units. The second unit starts working, while the main unit breaks for dinner. I start to realize there's no way for me to be in two places at once, so that means tonight will be filled with a lot of running back and forth.

6:30 PM. Second unit. Time to bring in the animals. For two of the transformation scenes, the Emohawk is seen turning into a toad and a chicken, which hop or fly away respectively. The toad will be shot in a few hours, but the chicken turns out to be more difficult than Bette Davis. All it has to do is fly away, but the bird refuses to move. Everything is tried, from loud noises, to cooing noises, to waving a large object behind it, to a finger creeping into shot just behind the chicken's backside. Nothing works.

The trainer finally suggests "what if we hold a piece of gut across, and walk it towards her?" A length of fishing line is located, held on both sides of the stubborn bird and dragged forward. To everyone's frustration, the chicken simply steps over it.

Finally, the frustrated trainer has one last suggestion. The camera rolls, coming in tight on the chicken. Behind it, a hand moves closer...and closer...contact! The chicken flies into the air with a great flurry of indignation. Mission accomplished, and the bruised bird goes off to phone its agent.

7:00 PM. Scene 19. The GELF chief has an Emohawk- a Polymorph. The camera is moved to the GELF cabin, and Ainsley is brought in. He looks like a giant orange Yeti. For the scene in which the Emohawk is seen for the first time, there's a cutaway shot of the GELF chieftain cradling the monster in one arm. While Kryten explains to his companions what an Emohawk is, the creature changes into several objects in rapid succession. That's what they're shooting now.

With Ainsley seated, a rabbit is brought in and seated in the crook of his arm. The animal is then removed and a table lamp is placed in the same spot. Freeze again, and the rabbit is placed on Ainsley's arm. He strokes it, with a massive hand that virtually envelopes the little creature.

The rabbit is again replaced by the lamp, which is then removed, to be replaced by a chinchilla. "Keep an eye on it," advises the trainer. "When it goes, it goes!" In the end, they decide not to film the chinch, and bring back the Emohawk puppet. Paul takes his position behind the GELF leader, and they record a shot of Ainsley feeding a worm to his hungry pet. The shot will eventually fill in both ends of the scene.

Main unit. Back in the GELF village (actually a medieval village built last year for the series Covington Cross) filming is ready to begin. Torches are lit in front of each of the huts, close to which several men dressed in hooded black robes are standing. Each of them is carrying a spear.

Among the hooded men is Time Out correspondent Bruce Dessau, who wrote last year's Red Dwarf Companion. He's having a ball playing an extra, although I don't see anything glamorous about standing in the back lot of Shepperton Studios freezing one's butt off. Then again. I'm the last one to talk!

The village is comprised of about a dozen thatched huts. In the square, a skeleton in a cage hangs from a gibbet. The huts are illuminated by carefully placed lights within.

The entrance to the village is a narrow bridge bordered by two idols, which crosses a narrow pond. One of the grips stirs the pond with a rake, but John Pomphrey tells him to be careful, or he'll damage the plastic. "You'll puncture the pond!" he laughs.

While they're waiting for the next shot, the cast members stand near the bridge, amusing themselves by doing impressions of Simon.

The floor manager takes it with good humor, but eventually asks them to stop. "How can I keep control when you keep doing that?"

7:15 PM. Just before the take, Andria and her assistants cross the bridge to blacken the robed figures' faces. They're all supposed to be GELFs, but since there's no money in the budget for a dozen hairy Yetis with two hours of prosthetic makeup, they're covered with the hooded robes so no one can see what they look like underneath.

Robert looks at a well-worn copy of this week's script. Tonight is a rough one for him. In addition to the usual expositional dialogue he has to recite, he also has several lines in GELF; a tongue-twisting language that seems to consist of clearing one's throat in various ways. Brandishing his script, he promises, 'I'm never going to complain about another line!"

7:45 PM. Scene 17. The crew make their way through the forest with their trunk of goods to trade with the GELFs.

Cat and Lister carry a large trunk containing items to trade with the GELFs. They're flanked by Kryten and Rimmer. On the other side of the bridge, they're surrounded by GELFs, who Kryten greets in their own language. The scene has to be done several times because of the difficult lighting conditions. After several attempts, Craig and Danny are getting visibly tired from carrying the trunk back and forth.

8:00 PM Second Unit. The animal wrangler brings in the stunt toad, and positions it on the table. She has to hold onto it to keep it from doing any unscheduled leaps. It's a big South American frog who waits for his big moment, then leaps high into the air. Obviously he's more of a professional than the chicken.

The camera is locked off, and Steve bends down behind the table. As the recording continues, he throws the plane into the cockpit. Unlike the transformations in 'Polymorph,' these changes may be enhanced with a tiny morph to make them more interesting, although the script does say NO MORPH.

8:15 PM. A hamster is brought in and placed on the floor. On cue, he scurries across the floor, not asking what his motivation for that scene is.

The camera is locked off again, and Springer the props buyer marks the appropriate spot. He brings in a pink slinky, which is supposed to- well, slink down a few steps to the mid-section. The action has to be repeated numerous times, first because the slinky won't go down the steps, and then because Springer's shadow is in shot. Finally, they get a half-decent take, and a small, radio controlled car is brought in to finish the sequence.

8:30 PM. Main unit. Scene 20. The GELF Chief concludes the wedding ceremony and hands over the O/G unit.

The action moves into the center of the square, where the wedding ceremony between Lister and his hairy bride will take place. Steve is wearing a bridal veil over his costume, and that probably helps, because most of the crew can't tell the GELFs apart. He's handed a huge bouquet of weeds which he holds upside down. Craig also has flowers added to his own hat.

Steve and Ainsley are joined by a third GELF for the ceremony. The actors are starting to get a bit smelly by now, and Howard tells me it's because the costumes are made from plumber's hemp; the material used to clean out drains. It's a shame the smell can't be recorded for television, as it contributes to the reality of the characters.

8:55 PM. The wedding scene takes some considerable time to record, because of the number of low-flying planes overhead. An annoyed Danny finally snaps, "How many fucking planes are there?" and Robert quips, "It must have something to do with Heathrow; I don't know, just a guess."

At this point, the cast is starting to get a bit punchy, as well as very cold. When Steve's bouquet hits Robert in the shoulder, he jokes, "A tree just fell on me!" A few minutes later, confetti is handed out to the cast for when the GELF bride kisses Lister. "Can I have some confetti?" asks Craig. "I'm going to marry a Yeti!"

9:25 PM. The second unit has already de-rigged and gone home, but here in the GELF village, filming continues very slowly. A few hundred yards away, another film crew is shooting a TV movie of MacGyver, and every so often, one of their crew members walks over to see what's happening. The sight of a wedding ceremony being held in a primitive village, with several hooded, spear-carrying figures as well as a strange-looking robot and a trio of hairy creatures must be fuel for a number of interesting stories on the neighboring location.

Craig is busy complaining to Rob and Doug about having to kiss two monsters this season: a Psiren and a GELF. "You haven't see episode six," Rob retorts, "the Lister-Rimmer kiss."

"Chris, we're going to French kiss in episode six," Craig tells his costar. Chris's response: "Rewrite!"

9:45 PM. Close-ups on the GELF chief.

10:10 PM. Scene 22. The crew leg it from the village. The GELF chief releases the Emohawk, which transmutes into a bird and follows them through the forest.

Of course the shot of Ainsley throwing the puppet into the air looks like...Ainsley throwing a puppet into the air. The shot will probably be cut down quite a bit, and the sound of wings flapping added for good measure.

10:30 PM. The bridge is cleared for Craig's escape. He runs from one end of the village, telling his companions, "Change of plans-leg it!" After several hours of freezing weather, I'm amazed that Craig has so much energy, and yet he manages several takes, each one of them good. After four runs, he collapses in mock exhaustion.

10:50 PM. Scene 23. The crew runs through the forest, making their way back to Starbug. They beat off the Emohawk, which is now a predatory bird.

The cast moves to a small clearing in the woods bordering on the village for the arrival of the Emohawk. Things continue to go wrong, as Danny recites his line perfectly, and then pauses, thinking he's blown it. When Craig tells him no, the line was correct, it's too late, and they have to do it over anyway.

11:30 PM. With several scenes still to be shot, a quick pizza break is called. Several pizzas arrive, and the crew stand around having a late snack. Kerry circulates, pouring brandy into people's coffee in an effort to keep warm. A fake campfire has been set up in the clearing- it's no more than an electric log, but people cluster around it as if it's a raging bonfire.

11:50 PM. The cast is called back into the woods for the rest of the scene. To simulate an arrow being shot into the trunk they're carrying, the arrow is imbedded in the trunk, and then pulled back on a length of fishing line. Again, the shot will be run backwards, making it look reasonably convincing.

12:10 AM. It's down to Robert's last line of the evening, or morning at this point The crew huddles around the tiny electric fire, waiting for that last line to be recorded, and then those magic words, "That's a wrap; thank you very much, everybody!"

Steve Wickham (GELF Bride), Ainsley Harriott (GELF Chief:

How did the two of you get the part of Gelfs in this episode?

Steve Wickham: I met the casting director about a year ago at a party, and she said if something came up in Red Dwarf that was right for me, she would give me a call.

Were they locking for a big guy to play the part?

Wickham:They thought about hiring extras for these parts, but because it's not easy and had to be acted even under layers of costume and makeup and speaking alien talk, you've still got to be able to act.

Ainsley Harriott: With me, like in most situations, you get a call from your agent, and when you realize it's Red Dwarf, you know it's got quite a cult attached to it, and you think, "Yeah, I'd like to do something like that!" I have to admit I'm not part of the whole cult movement actually, but I do enjoy watching it.

At what point did you find out what you were going to be wearing for the part?

Wickham: We didn't actually see them until Thursday when we had to put them on.

Harriott: That was extraordinary. It took about two and a half hours sitting in costume and makeup, as you see yourself change, and the only bit that you actually recognize-or the only bit that my mother will recognize is my eyes and say, "That's my boy!"

How uncomfortable were they to wear?

Harriott: It was just quite cold hanging around, and you do tend to hang around quite a lot, but wardrobe did a fantastic job.

Wickham: It's a body suit then a strap-on stomach, so it wasn't uncomfortable to wear. It's just the face mask which is constricting.

What was the most fun about doing it?

Wickham: They're so good at what they do.

Harriott: The characters are so well formed. They know exactly what they're doing, and it definitely rubs off on the rest of the crew: the camera men, the sound people; everybody. They know what they're doing, and you can just slot yourself into it, and it's wonderful.

It must have been even more tedious in your case, where you had all the second unit effects that had to be done, such as keeping your hand still for the Emohawk transformations.

Harriott: It's all part of the job. They had that chinchilla which they didn't put in there, because that would have really been interesting: to see it scamper off, and we'd have to do it all over.

I notice when you put your hand over that rabbit, it seemed to disappear.

Harriott: You know how it is with us aliens: we're great at covering things up!

Wickham: I was told by the lady from the magazine that we're not aliens; we're GELFs: genetically-engineered life forms.

Harriott: Fair enough; we're GELFS. My apologies. It's very gratifying in fact when the producer turned around, and I think other people had mentioned it to him that we were undoubtedly the best monster-type characters they've had in the series, so that in itself was very encouraging. It makes you want to do your part well. You originally go in with that intention anyway, but to get a few words of encouragement is marvelous. It gives you that extra kick.

Wickham: It's just a buzz to be involved in a popular cult program.

Is it difficult to have a part where A) you're not going to be speaking a known language, and B) you're not going to be seen under all the makeup?

Harriott: From my own personal view, it's rather difficult as an actor in the present climate. There's not a lot of work around, so if you get an opportunity, it's a case of not only taking the opportunity but getting out there and mixing with people in the business. That's actually what brings work about a lot of the time. If you're able to play the part well, people think they might use you again, and they might be producers or directors, so that could actually help you in your career. I don't think it's a negative thing at all.

Saturday, March 20. Audience Recording Day: 'Polymorph II: Emohawk.'

3:00 PM. Rehearsals are going very smoothly today. For the first time this season, an auto cue has been installed just outside the cockpit set which will certainly make things go very quickly. Because of the lateness of this week's script the cast hasn't had as much time to learn their lines properly, so the mere presence of an auto cue, particularly for Robert's long expositional speeches, should make a difference.

The high point of today's rehearsals is the scene between Lister and his new bride, as "she" tries to interest him in a little wedding night activity. What makes it so funny is that both actors are dressed in civilian clothes, so the sight of the massive Steve trying to seduce Craig are extremely funny.

4:45 PM. A problem that may crop up tonight is that the mid-section air lock doors aren't opening properly or on cue. After several bumps and bruises, Craig arranges a sound cue with Mel's stage hands to open the doors at a certain point.

5:00 PM. Danny pops his buck teeth in to rehearse his scenes as Duane. It's interesting to watch how his personality changes when he wears the teeth. Of course tonight he'll have all the props, including the classic Duane wardrobe, as well as thermos, lunch box and several items of Duane-related paraphernalia.

Chris on the other hand, is having a bit more difficulty playing Ace this time. He's still in his standard Rimmer costume, plus the original Ace wig has been lost between seasons four and six. He's not as happy with the new wig, or the script, which only has a few minutes of Ace almost as an after thought.

7:30 PM. With this season's filming rapidly drawing to a close, much of today has to be spent doing interviews with cast and crew members who have been too busy during the last few weeks.

The biggest hold-out so far has been Howard Burden, who has had a tremendous amount of work to do these last few months, with relatively little lime to do it. He finally agrees that once the cast is dressed for tonight's recording, he'll have some much-needed free time.

Walking into the wardrobe department just outside stage G is a strange experience. It's like a giant closet, filled with virtually every Red Dwarf costume for the last several years. On one rack, I see one of Cat's belts, Rimmer's blue and red costumes, and a pair of concubine masks from Rimmerworld . There are also several pieces of Roman armor, Lister's shabby long johns and his silver space jacket.

Piled on the floor and on another rack are the black robes used for this weeks extras. Beneath the rack are a pair of simulant boots, cowboy boots, and several pairs of shoes used during the black and while scenes of 'Gunmen.' Some of them are already packed away in BBC plastic bags to be returned.

To the left of Howard's cluttered desk is a spare room filled with racks of costumes. I see Legion's mask, the cube Kryten, spare

Kryten parts, and several pairs of AR boots stacked against the wall. Another rack holds several Cat costumes, Legion's green outfit, and a bunch of other costumes from various episodes.

While Howard and I are talking, we can see the recording on a closed circuit monitor piped into the wardrobe department. Until now, I was never sure how the designer knew when there was a crisis on the studio floor, but it soon becomes obvious that he can do several different things while keeping an eye on the monitor.

8:30 PM. Tonight's recording goes fairly smoothly, thanks in large part I think, to the auto cue. By having Robert's speeches on screen, the early cockpit scenes go by very quickly.

My favorite moment of the night has to be a scene in the mid-section, with Rimmer, Cat and Kryten. Rimmer tells the others that virtually everything of value has been destroyed by Starbug's crash landing. After he leaves, Kryten picks up a guitar. "At least Mr. Lister's guitar survived intact," he tells Cat, who grabs the instrument, smashes it and hands it back. "Not even Mr. Lister's guitar survived intact," Kryten corrects himself.

That's what was supposed to happen. In a wonderful blooper, Kryten tells the Cat, "At least Mr. Guitar..." He realizes his mistake at the same time as the audience, who roar with laughter. Robert and Danny look at each other? "Mr. Guitar?" they repeat, and break into spontaneous song, "Oh Mr. Guitar..." with Robert strumming on the still-intact instrument. "You see, for me everything is Mr.," he tells the audience. "Mr. Cat," he continues pointing to his costar. "Mr. Microphone," and then pointing to his groinal area, "Mr. Rather Sad Knob." The correct take isn't nearly as funny.

10:10 PM. Towards the end of the night, Danny goes out in the corridor outside Stage G. He's just finished his last scene as Duane, and still dressed in his best Dibley Wear, he regales the fans with his new Duane Dance; a wonderful bit that puts Pee Wee Herman's old Big Shoe Dance to shame. For the fans who couldn't get in to the studio and had to watch the recording on a monitor tonight, it's an unexpected treat.

Tonight's recording ends a bit late; nothing new for this season of Red Dwarf. The cast take their bows and everyone heads for the bar. Next week is the final chunk of recording, but it's going to be a difficult one.

Tuesday, March 23. Rehearsal Day: 'Present From the Future.'

1:00 PM. With only a few days left in production, there are still a lot of interviews to be done for the book, which means spending as much time in the studio as possible. Although Justin has discouraged me from attending rehearsal days (they're really for the artists and director, he points out), he agrees that today and tomorrow would be good days for getting a few interviews.

At the moment, the cast is rehearsing the second draft of 'Present From the Future,' previously called 'Time And Time Again,' although I don't think that title ever made it to a final script. Also present are Andy, Mel and Rina, who jots down any possible corrections in the script.

The mood on the set isn't the best I've seen in the last several weeks. The cast has only had a day with the script, which means they haven't had much time to learn their lines. There have been a few strained moments between cast and production team, and while I don't know all the specifics, there are plenty of hints as to what's been happening.

One major problem is that Friday has been designated as a pick-up day, where shots from the first six episodes can be re-shot. A production office bulletin board is covered with post-it notes from Rob, Doug, Andy and Justin as to which scenes should be redone.

What this means is that the cast loses a day of rehearsal time in order to re-shoot those other scenes. It also means that Robert has to suffer through an extra day in Kryten makeup, and he's desperately unhappy about it. By this time in the season, he doesn't count recording time by the number of days, but rather by the number of masks he has to wear. Until now, that mean two "mask days," but now there are three.

1:30 PM. Scene 13. Everyone objects to a line where Kryten says, "I'm terribly sorry sirs, my Mawkish mode appears to have gone into overdrive." "It's a bit seersucker, doesn't it?" comments Andy. Craig suggests "saccharine mode," while Robert suggests "male bonding mode." The discussion then goes into where the auto cue will go during the recording on Thursday. Without it, the day could be a very long one.

2:00 PM. Scene 14. The other cast members joke around with Craig, who thinks his future self won't be seen. Perhaps he can phone it in. Craig is not amused.

Rehearsals are interrupted by the arrival of stand-up comic and Red Dwarf guest star Tony Hawks. "Just thought I'd pop in and give you a few notes," says Hawks, who is busy filming a commercial on the adjoining stage. The cast is pleasantly surprised to see him again. Hawks had done a number of guest shots in the series, either in person or as a voice-over.

2:30 PM. Craig is starting to get even more upset that this is the last episode of the season, and he's playing a brain in a jar. Naturally, his co-stars are extremely unhelpful. "Don't worry," says Andy, "they've promised to put in 20 more gags by tonight. "Twenty more feed lines!" counters Danny.

2:45 PM. Robert suggests the idea of shooting the episode on Thursday and Friday, and showing it to the audience on Saturday. One can almost see him thinking, "Then I don't have to wear the mask three times." Andy says it would be too difficult to edit the episode by Saturday, but he suggests trying to shoot as much as possible on Thursday. At least that would make the final recording day easier.

3:00 PM. Andy tries to choreograph the big death scenes. There's a discussion about cast members being in different places on the ship, but Andy quite rightly points out that they should all be together for the final battle.

4:30 PM. Scene 19. Craig suggests adding “stretch me neck” to his line “It’s nice to get out for a change, get a bit of air.” Andy tells Rina to pencil it in.

4:45 PM. Word comes down from the production office that a third draft of the script will have significant changes in dialogue. Chris points out that this makes rehearsals useless at this point- why keep going over lines that are going to be changed shortly? Andy sends for Justin, who calls Rob and Doug at their office in London. Finally, a compromise is reached: they’ll break for today, and the next draft of the script will be messengered to each cast member early this evening. The director asks them to make an effort to memorize their lines for tomorrow’s rehearsal.

Wednesday, March 24. Rehearsal Day: ‘Present From the Future.’

11:15 AM. Most of my day is spent doing interviews, although I sit down to watch the tech run at 3:00. This is a run-through where members of the technical crew are present to note any potential problems, or to answer any questions. Present are the cast, Andy, Peter Wragg, Paul McGuiness, production assistant Chrissie Moses, Kerry, Mel, Steve, Dai, Jeff, Rocket and John Pomphrey.

It soon becomes obvious that this week has been difficult for the crew as well. Costume, makeup and set design have only had a few days to work on the script, which has already been through three drafts. When Chris says his line, “Its no secret that morale’s on the floor,” there’s a healthy burst of laughter from almost everyone present. At least no one has lost his sense of humor.

Thursday, March 25. Pre-VT Day: ‘Present From the Future.’

9:45 AM. The normal Thursday rush, as set, prop and FX people struggle to get the cockpit and mid-section sets ready for filming. The auto cue girl is busily typing lines into her computer, and a monitor is wheeled into the mid-section so the cast members will be able to see their lines.

10:00 AM. Scene 19. Kryten meets the future members of the Future Crew and Lister's brain.

Chris, Danny and Robert appear on the set, as their characters' future selves. Danny, as the aging Cat, is wearing a bald cap with long stringy gray hair, a padded belly, and his tartan jacket from last season.

Chris is also well-padded, with red velvet pants, a yellow jacket trimmed with red, and a gray wig and beard. Tim English joins them on the stage, dressed in Kryten makeup and costume. He'll be doubling for Robert for some of the complicated split screen sequences today. At first glance, he looks just like Robert, but a closer examination reveals a different person under the mask.

A few moments later, Robert walks in, a terrible- looking toupee and bushy eyebrows added to his Kryten mask. He is wearing a powder blue suit, white shoes, a white turtleneck and a medallion around his neck.

Finally, Lister's brain is brought in- an eerily realistic brain, floating in a glass jar. The brain has been made by an outside contractor booked by Howard Burden, rather than the FX department. Howard fanned out the job when Lister's body was meant to be housed in a robotic body of some kind, but when the idea was changed at the last minute, the same company continued to make the brain instead.

10:25 AM. Scene 19. Kryten meets the three members of the future crew and Lister's brain. Robert's double opens airlock to admit future crew. This scene will probably get the biggest laugh on Saturday. The three cast members look marvelous, but it's actually the brain that will cause a few problems. A good deal of time is spent discussing how it will be carried and eventually introduced on camera.

10:40 AM. Ready for first take. Danny adds a bit where he combs his hair while entering, and looks at several hairs stuck in his comb.

It's a funny moment, but if there are too many takes, he stands a good chance of losing his remaining hairs.

After the take, Chris steps off the stage and sits down in the front row of bleachers next to me. I ask him how he feels about all the padding. "It's fine," he says, "but a bit warm."

11:00 AM. Lister's brain is revealed. As Kryten pulls the cover off the jar, the brain can be seen floating inside the liquid. A blinking yellow light has been attached to the jar to give it an even stranger look.

11:50 AM. Chris films his close-ups for the monitor. I sit with Andria and Robert, who are talking about the problems the crew is having with Lister's brain. We all agree the gag would be a lot funnier if Craig's head had been in the jar instead, while the brain's gag potential is limited. Robert says the brain will get at least one big laugh, when it's revealed.

I say wouldn't it be funnier if Craig's plaits were actually on the jar? Andria's eyes light up. She runs over to get approval from Rob and Doug, and gives me a thumbs up. A few minutes later, she returns from the makeup room with an extra set of Craig's locks, which are then glued to the jar.

12:15 PM. Craig arrives, in full costume and makeup. Although strictly speaking, he isn't actually in this scene, he still has to read the lines for his brain in the jar. Peter the "brain wrangler" crouches behind the table, synchronizing the jar's blinking lights with the dialogue.

Meanwhile, James Davis is busy in the cockpit, wiring up the set for the climactic battle sequence. He lays duplicate charges to speed up possible retakes later on. The only problem with that he tells me, is that one charge can't be too close to another, or it sets the second charge off as well. One has to be very careful to know where everything is.

12:35 PM. I wander outside for a cup of coffee and see Howard standing outside the wardrobe department, having a cigarette. He's very relieved that the week is almost over. This week's script changes have caused him a lot of headaches. Originally, Craig was going to be a short, Robbie the Robot character, but that was changed to the brain in a jar. For another sequence, the producers wanted four moose heads for the cast members, which couldn't be done on such short notice. The next best thing was to get four different animal heads, which is what he did.

12:45 PM. Lister/the brain's entrance. So far, the rest of the scene has been going pretty well, thanks in large part to the auto cue's presence.

In the ops room, Paul is putting the finishing touches on Lister's robotic arm, which is needed for an earlier scene. The foam arm has been sliced open, and filled with bits of wire and machine parts. The edges of the wound are then re-sealed, as though the arm has been melted open.

1:15 PM. The future crew leaves Starbug, punctuated by blasts from Lister's bazookoid. Small charges have been planted along the airlock wall, making the blasts much more realistic. In all likelihood, electronic effects will also be added in post-production.

1:30 PM. The crew breaks for lunch. Mel and Peter's teams confer with Rob, Doug and Andy about redoing the Star Drive scene from 'Call Me Legion;' one of the scenes slated for tomorrow's pick-up day. Rob and Doug actually want the device to rip free of its moorings, with hoses and cables flying. The group is joined by Justin, and they go into the engine room set to discuss the scene.

2:30 PM. Robert gets back into his Kryten costume, while his double changes into future Kryten's suit and wig. Andy will now shoot him from the back to complete the scene. While Tim is in makeup, Simon puts on the jacket himself and stands in for Robert for a pick-up shot of Lister's brain.

3:30 PM. The previous scene is now filmed in reverse, with Robert missing as the present-day Kryten. The second pass mattes his character in on both sides of the shot.

4:00 PM. There are some problems with the second pass. Because the camera has gone so far into the shot, it is now very difficult to keep the lights from throwing a boom shadow across the set. John Pomphrey and Ron Green spend quite a long time trying to get rid of the offending shadow so that filming can resume.

5:05 PM. Scene 4. Kryten examines Lister's injured arm. They see he has a robotic arm, and X rays reveal that he is a droid.

In order to create the illusion of Lister's arm being torn open, the crew uses Craig's sleeve and vest, while the actor stands a few feet away. Paul stands in for Robert, wearing Kryten's gloves, and tears the sleeve open for the camera, revealing mechanics and blinking lights.

5:15 PM. Danny returns to the set, wearing this week's Cat costume, including a black, blue and red checked fringed leather jacket. He's worried that the sleeves aren't the right length, and walks around the set, asking people's opinion. There isn't much sympathy to be had.

5:25 PM. While Kryten sits at the table, Rimmer and Cat come down the stairs. These elements will be matted in with other shots of Lister and the future crew.

5:45 PM. A large green cloth has been erected on the left side of the stage, covering the wall and floor. This will be used for a green screen sequence later on. The cockpit seats are dismantled and placed in front of the cloth.

Back in the mid-section, Craig is brought in for his close-up on the gantry. He fires his bazookoid, for the final element in the shot, and the crew breaks for dinner.

7:55 PM. The cast reassembles in the ops room, where they'll be hoisted on bunks into the air. Peter, James and Paul pull on a series of weights in order to raise and lower the platform. Craig and Danny get on one bunk; Chris on the other, and Andy calls for rehearsal.

The bunk with Craig and Danny is raised and then lowered, while smoke fills the chamber. When the platform hits bottom, several members of the crew venture off-color conclusions as to what the two actors were doing in the sleep cabinet.

8:05 PM. Scene 10. The crew go into the deep sleep units. Kryten seals Lister and Cat into one of the hibernation bunks. The scene is done over and over, with Peter and his crew getting more tired with each take. It's a lot of weight for three men to handle.

8:45 PM. When that sequence is finished, Craig and Danny get off the bunk, and Chris sits down. Robert gets in beside him. With a bit of editing, it will appear that both bunks are movable instead of just the first one.

9:15 PM. Scene 26. They attack Future Starbug crew and hit them. The Future crew return laser fire and damage Starbug badly. After several hits, they all lie dead except for Rimmer.

Andy gets ready to run through the final battle scene. "Ready to rehearse- no pyros!" Simon announces. Peter and his crew surround the cockpit, ready to activate the charges. Doug does not like the shot. "It's too funny!" he tells Andy, referring to Chris's shaking of Kryten. "You've got to make it real, you've got to go for the drama!"

9:45 PM. Doug asks Andy to record a scene without the explosions, although the director doesn't think it will be easy. He suggests recording a rehearsal instead. The take is okay, but Doug is still not convinced. He now thinks Danny's death looks too funny.

9:50 PM. Ready to record. Peter's team makes a few last-minute adjournments. Complete silence on the set. Major explosions. Craig's death looks terrific, and docs Danny's. Sitting directly behind Rob and Doug in the first row of the bleachers, I tell them it's a wonderful scene. In a way, it's almost too bad the episode couldn't end on that note. They both agree; it's like the final episode of Blake's 7.

10:00 PM. After the scene, virtually die entire cast and crew want to see the retake, but the monitors have been turned off. Everyone clusters around a tiny black and white camera monitor to see the replay. It looks impressive. There's a loud murmur of approval, and the crew packs up their gear to go home.

Friday, March 26. Pick-Up Day: Episodes 1-6

For the cast and crew, it was business as usual, but with a lot of costume changes. Just for the record, these are the scenes that were scheduled for re-shoots:

'Psirens'

Scene 25. The temptresses have been re-cast with two new actresses. [Ultimately the scene that airs is the original]

Scenes 24/26/27/28. The Captain Tau/Kochanski scenes have to be tightened up with shots of the boys in the studio.

Scene 50. Cube Kryten looking over the edge. Original is unconvincing.

'Call Me Legion'

Scenes 30, 32. Star Drive explodes out of the ship, and the gang hangs on for dear life. The Star Drive itself has to be re-shot to look more convincing, while the vacuum shot has to be re-staged with Rimmer in his hard light costume.

'Rimmerworld'

Scenes 19/21/25. Escape Pod sequences.

Scene 2. Lister's line, "...Maybe some good news..."

Scene 7. Simulant ship corridor scene. Original is too dark too really see what's happening. It was shot at the end of the day, in too much of a hurry.

Scene 11. Corridor again. See above.

'Gunmen of the Apocalypse'

An exterior shot of doves flying. The originals had their wings clipped, so flying was the last thing on their minds. The yee-hah! Scene. Obviously the boys hadn't seen City Slickers yet, and their yee-hah just didn't cut it.

'Present From the Future'

Scene 13. Lister and Kryten fit the time drive.

Scene 7. No Cat shot and animal head shot.

Scene 17. Kryten oversees other crew docking.

Scene 27. Rimmer destroys the Time Drive.

Scene 26. The climactic death scene.

Scene/Page	Set/Description	Cast/Artists	Costume/Make-up	Cameras	Notes

RED DWARF VI : PICK-UPS

PICK-UPS RUNNING ORDER : FRIDAY 26TH MARCH 1993

SHOOT: 10.00 - 13.00 LUNCH: 13.00 -14.00 CONTINUE: 14.00 - 18.00
SUPPER: 18.00 - 19.00 CONTINUE: 19.00 - 22.00

7	RIMMERWORLD INT. SIMULANT SHIP CORRIDOR Kryten announces that the Bazookoids can't be used should they encounter the simulants because the noise could cause a tremor which would finally destroy the ship. Rimmer panics even more.	Kryten Cat Lister Rimmer			Burnt-out machi-nery. Psi-Scan Bazook-oids Rimmer's Hard Light Belt.
11	RIMMERWORLD INT. SIMULANT SHIP CORRIDOR Simulant POV of Lister, Cat and Kryten.	Lister Cat Kryten			Psi-Scan Bazook-oids Debris
25	PSIRENS CUSHIONY CURTAINY AREA Two beautiful temptresses appear on the monitor begging for help as their settlement is almost extinct. They need see spreaders.	Temptress 1 Temptress 2			Wind Machine

Some of these scenes weren't finished during yesterday's filming, while others are being re-shot, tightened up or generally improved. This schedule was entirely subject to time constraints, although certain scenes did have priority. Since I'll be interviewing Rob, Doug and Andy tomorrow for the book, I'm sure I'll hear about which ones were successes, and which ones never made.

Saturday, March 27. Audience Recording Day: 'Present From the Future.'

1:00 PM. Rehearsals start on the last day of the final episode of Red Dwarf VI. Robert is wearing a pair of very dark sunglasses, not because he's hung-over but from his eyes being terribly sensitive. Having to wear the Kryten makeup two days in a row has taken its toll on him.

The others are in good spirits, as compared to the mood of a few days ago. Chris in particular, is in a very good mood. Danny is carrying around a huge cigar; possibly to celebrate the birth of a new series?

Today is a bit of a blur for me to. There's a lot of last- minute interviews to do. I talk to Rob and Doug over lunch and Andy during the dinner break. In-between, I try to get all the last-minute comments I couldn't get from people during the last six weeks. People have always been happy to talk once they got used to the idea of my being there, but a few balked at speaking into a tape recorder.

There is one memory of today that I will remember for a long time. After a run-through of the final scene today, I tell Rob and Doug that it's a bit of a cheat. For two parents who have just been told their baby is ugly, they take it rather well, and ask me why. I tell them the scene is missing any reference to Red Dwarf. Having spent the last six episodes trying to find their lost ship I ask, shouldn't there at least be at least a one-line mention of it? They nod their heads, no doubt thinking, "Who the hell is this guy anyway, and why did we ever ask him to write a book about our show?"

A few hours later, the writers walk up to me, holding out two yellow rewrite pages of the final scene. In it, Kryten mentions the fact that they've relocated Red Dwarf's vapor trail, and are barely six days behind. Score one for the obnoxious American.

Sc. 28 INT. MID-SECTION

LISTER, **CAT** AND **RIMMER** AROUND THE SCANNER TABLE. **KRYTEN** ENTERS FROM GALLEY WITH TRAY.

```
KRYTEN
Well, sirs, as you know, this
is the best drink we've got
on board.  It's the wine I
brewed from urine re-cyc, we
have much to celebrate Mr
Rimmer destroyed the Time
Drive.  Deleted our future
selves and saved us all.

RIMMER
Kryten please its not
something I'm proud of.

KRYTEN
Furthermore we've relocated
Red Dwarf's vapour trail and
are barely six days behind.
May I take the liberty of
proposing a toast.
```

*Lost scenes: The original ending to 'Present from the Future.' After Rimmer destroys the Time Drive, the crew reconvenes in the mid-section. This ending was replaced by the season-ending cli*ffhanger of Starbug exploding.

LISTER, CAT and RIMMER around the scanner table. KRYTEN enters from galley with tray.

*KRYTEN: Well, sirs, as you know, this is the best drink we've got on board. It's the wine I brewed from urine re-cyc. We have much to cele*brate. Mr. Rimmer destroyed the time Drive. Deleted our future selves and saved us all.

RIMMER: Kryten, please, it's not something I'm proud of.

*KRYTEN: Furthermore, we've relocated Red Dwarf's vapor trail and are barely six days behind. May I take the liber*ty of proposing a toast.

They each take a glass. They raise glasses.

KRYTEN: To the present!

ALL: The present.

They drink.

ALL (Ad lib): Nice wine… good year…best yet.

(Run credits)

…

The audience recording is full of mixed emotion for the cast and crew. There's a lot of tiredness and a little sadness. Lots of delight at finally finishing the last episode. Over the last week or two, a few people have told me they probably won't be coming back for another season (if there is one) but tonight, those feelings have been forgotten.

After tonight's recording, the cast and crew reassemble in another part of Shepperton Studios for the cast party. Virtually everyone involved in making the series this year has been invited, so I see lots of guest stars from different episodes, including Steve (the GELF) bride) Wickham, and Stephen Marcus, who played Bearstrangler McGee. Sheelagh arrives in time to go to the party, which gives me the chance to introduce her to some of the crew members she's been hearing about for two months but hasn't met.

While Sheelagh chats with a few of the FX boys, Lois Burwell walks up to me, gives me a big hug and hands me a small brown paper bag. I open the bag to find it's full of hair: Craig's plaits, which have been cut off after tonight's filming. They're sealed in to his own hair at the beginning of each season, and he normally cuts them off in front of the audience at the last recording. I had asked Andria and Lois if they would save the hair for me, as I've been invited to a

Red Dwarf convention in Leicester tomorrow, and it would a nice addition to the charity auction.

Unfortunately, Craig decided tonight that he didn't want to undergo the usual haircut in front of several hundred Red Dwarf fans, so that was that. It therefore comes as a surprise when Lois hands me the bag, complete with two Polaroid's of Craig triumphantly cutting off his hair in the makeup room.

Speaking of Craig, he's spent the last few hours walking around the party with a small naked replica of himself. It's the statue that was created for 'Timeslides,' seen as a giant peeing fountain. Rocky had promised it to Craig, and true to his word, he presents him with it at the party.

Because I have to travel up to Leicester early tomorrow morning, our presence at the party has to be cut short. I spend the next half hour trying to find people and say good-bye. It's a difficult thing to do. In two weeks, I'll be sitting down at my computer back in New Jersey, and all this will become a memory. I feel a very genuine sense of loss that I probably won't see any of these people again. All I can do is try and write a book that will try to put those thoughts on paper. That ends my time with the cast and crew of Red Dwarf VI. As the saying goes, I can't wait to read the book…

Interviews

Chris Barrie (Rimmer)

What brought you back this season?

Chris Barrie: I don't really know. To honest, at the time when I was doing the fifth series, I didn't really want to do a sixth series, but of course as time unfolds, you forget, so when it came around to the sixth, I thought well, it's not that bad after all, and I need to break up the year a bit from doing commercials and things. Plus the thing of having two shows at the same time, this and 'Brittas' sort of grabbed me and made me feel it's nice to keep two shows on the go. But I forgot about the sheer frustration and pain that goes into making this series. I thought the production people have had a chance to sort it out in series five, and they'll have learned by their mistakes and take those lessons on into six, so it will be like a normal television program, but as we speak, they haven't, and here I am again.

What were some of the problems you had?

Barrie: I think when this series goes onto the screen, it will probably look fine, but I think it could have turned out better if it had been properly executed. I hasten to add here, we're not talking about the technicians, the artists and the actual creative side; not even the writing. We're talking about the actual organization. It's lacking one dynamic figure which it had in the first four series to put it on to tape: Ed Bye.

Did you feel that Andy was able to find his feet on the series as director?

Barrie: I think Andy is a fantastic young director, and I mean that, because you can't be anything else to survive what he did. He found his feet at the end, because he was allowed to find his feet then. He would have found his feet within the first two weeks had he been allowed, but he just wasn't allowed. But he plugged on; that's the kind of bloke he is, and whatever differences he and I might have had were not because of. . . the differences that we had, were because of the situation, the circumstances that made tempers flair in that situation on a couple of occasions. I've worked with Andy on Spitting Image from the days he was painting puppets, and I know what kind of bloke he is, and I think he did bloody well to do all that on Red Dwarf. It's a very difficult situation. People who feel that strongly about their own scripts should either direct them themselves, or just go right away from it and let a strong director, or someone like Andy get on with it.

What was it like as an actor to be able to touch things again?

Barrie: Touching again was just a relief, because Rimmer never touched. That was a bit frustrating, but now we've got the hard light drive, it's good to be able to lean on things without fans writing in and saying, "Oh, Rimmer touched this, that and the other!" It's just a nice thing not to have to go through those gear changes.

What did you think about **'**Gunmen?**'** It seems to be the favorite.

Barrie: Without having seen the final cut, if it's all done the way my mind's eye sees it, I think it should be as good as some of the best episodes the show has ever produced. We had a great day for that western stuff, and if the post-production is good enough on it, it should look pretty spectacular. I really loved the fight scene, and the horse stuff was fine as well (apart from when Danny went "Yee hah!" at the end, and I nearly went into the back of that coach), but apart from that, it was good fun.

How did you feel about riding a horse?

Barrie: It was interesting in that respect. I was nervous; ultimately I think if they're wise, they'll not make it the horse show, they'll just use the horses when required, in terms of making the program. Yeah, it was nerve wracking, but the longer I was on the horse, the better it was.

Whose voice were you doing in that? It sounded a bit like Reagan.

Barrie: A bit of Reagan, a bit of Clint thrown in there. The way I was looking at it was to try and get the coolness of Clint across, and it sort of came out as my impression of Reagan, really. It wasn't any specific thing, just one of those cool, slightly smarter sort of cowboys than your average ones.

How easy was it to choreograph the fight scene?

Barrie: We spent a goodly amount of time getting it right, and thanks to Gerard and his stuntmen, we worked at it long and hard, and I kept thinking of things to do, so I'll be watching that more than anything else in the post-production to see what they've done with it.

It's interesting that **'Rimmerworld'** is probably the one where your character got the most to do, and yet you don't seem to regard it that highly.

Barrie: It seemed to remind me of other stories. 'Rimmerworld' felt a lot like 'Terrorform' to me. That could have been another title for it. That was visiting Rimmer's psyche, but that did make me go "Wow." You had the two sides of Rimmer, the good and the bad. and I thought that one was really nice, where 'Rimmerworld' looked a bit plot-y; it didn't make me… to be fair, I've got to wait until I see them to make the final decision, but… I just thought 'Rimmerworld' immediately smacked of Terrorform,' where you're on a planet with lots of dry ice, and there's lots of Rimmers around. Maybe that was country that was visited before in a better way, I don't know.

How did you feel about the return of Ace?

Barrie: I would have liked to pre-record most of Ace, in order to get it absolutely right, and I would have liked the uniform back. I think the bits that we did do were all right, but it was a small little thing that wasn't that Ace-y to do, really. Ace likes to be flying about in spaceships and doing really dynamic things, and I don't think the full dynamism of the character exploited in 'Emohawk.' It was nice to be able to do the voice again, and flick back the hair, but it's a character I'd like to do a lot more with, maybe a whole series.

Were you glad you got to do the character again, or would you rather have done him only if he had been done properly?

Barrie: I don't think Ace fully came back. I think he came back in voice and spirit, but I don't think it was as clever a use of Ace as it could have been. I don't know, I was just disappointed that we didn't have the same wig, which was apparently stolen, and the same outfit. With 'Dimension Jump' in the fourth series, the wig and the outfit were so right and so wonderful. I could walk past to the studio and people would think it was my natural hair. It was the physicality of it, so that got me down a bit.

Was it harder to get back into the character again without all of that?

Barrie: A little bit, yes. It's a very fine thing, and it's in no way Andria or Howard's or anyone's fault: it's just that we didn't have the right stuff at our disposal, and it wasn't ever going to be quite as good. What Ace had to say was fine; in many ways, it was worth doing it for the Bambi gag. Put it this way: if I had one criticism, I think his entrance to tire scenario at that point could have been a little more dramatic. Maybe if we had pre-recorded it, it might have been better.

Dramatic or funny?

Barrie: Dramatic dash funny. It was a bit sort of nothing. It wasn't a very powerful entrance, but it was like because Rimmer became Ace, whereas Ace should have made his made his entrance real powerful and cool. Ace himself is not a desperately funny character. It's funny that he's Rimmer's other-dimensional sort of thing, but for Ace to work, it really has to be cool at all times, and it took a while for his coolness to get going.

What do you think the highlights for this series are going to be?

Barrie: That's a difficult question to answer, really. When I see it go out, the shows will probably have a completely different character, because there's two months editing or whatever, and they'll make the shows up then. I think the highlights for this series have to be 'Gunmen of the Apocalypse' and' Emohawk,' particularly 'Gunmen.'

That was actually a highlight in any performer's career, getting to saddle up and fiddle around with guns in a Western village. Some of the earliest images you see on television are Westerns with John Wayne, Gary Cooper, and people like that, so just to be able to don all those outfits was a great experience. We were kids again.

What would you have liked to have seen this time that there wasn't time to do?

Barrie: More time for rehearsal, basically. I think the scripts as they stand, a lot of them have been very good, but it's obviously harder when you've done 30 episodes to do another six and keep the stories as spicy and fresh as ever. It would have been nice to have had the scripts earlier to be able to think about them; I think that goes for the whole production, and just have more rehearsal time. The show has really become more of a visual effects show I think, and we performers tend to be feeding the visual effects.

Craig Charles (Lister)

What's been harder about this series than the others?

Craig Charles: Just dealing with a production that doesn't seem to know what it's doing. The left hand doesn't seem to know what the right hand is doing. Everything's supposed to make it easy to concentrate on your performance on screen, and nothing's made easy for you here.

Does that make you have to work that much harder?

Charles: Oh yeah, especially playing a chirrupy, optimistic kind of character and you're in a pit of depression because of the way things have been handled. Of course you have to notch up.

What have the positive aspects of this series so far?

Charles: I think it's going to be great to look at. There's some funny episodes. I think 'Gunmen of the Apocalypse' is going to be spectacular.

Do you think that was the highlight of the series?

Charles: I don't know, I think Dwayne Dibbly might steal the series again.

I mean for you personally.

Charles: I think 'Gunmen of the Apocalypse' was a good one. I think 'Psirens' was a good one for me, and 'Legion' was quite good.

Do you think the cast has rallied together again?

Charles: We're getting on better than we've ever got on, which is quite nice. It's a case of you're doing night shoots in the freezing cold and no one brings a heater. You find yourself next to a hut with a warm light.

I was amazed by how much energy you still had in those scenes.

Charles: You've got to put the performance on screen, because at the end of the day, that's what all the money has paid for. That's what it's all about: the four of us on screen, and you've got to do it. You can't let it affect your job, however it would be nice if they could make it easier rather than harder. And the scripts have been very late this year.

But you're very quick at picking it up.

Charles: I think I'm the quickest of the guys at learning lines, but even then, once you've leaned the lines, you have to start toying with how you're going to say them. We didn't get this script until Wednesday f**king morning, and it's Thursday now. I suppose it's not Rob and Doug's fault. They've been working hard, but they've got to sort the budget things out on this.

Has it stopped being fun for you?

Charles: No, I've had fun. It's been fun in different areas. It's been fun hanging out with the cast, and we've had a good laugh, but there's been a lot of hypocrisy and underhandedness and duplicity and double dealing, which takes the edge and shine off it, I suppose.

But you've had some pretty good moments.

Charles: I've had some good scenes. My part is getting back to where it should be now. It's more like the first couple of series now than it was last year. It's starting to revolve around me a little more.

Is that because of Hattie not being in it?

Charles: Hattie didn't have much to say last year. She had the occasional line.

Did that change the dynamics this year, not having her here?

Charles: I miss her, but she wasn't happy just doing what she was doing. She either had to have more to say or nothing to say, really. She wasn't happy with just six lines an episode.

Did you feel this series was funny?

Charles: Yeah, in a different way. It's very formulated, with the same lines every week. That's it, we're deader than tank tops, we're deader than corduroy. This week is just a no show. I could have phoned it in. It's weird, watching them sit around the mid-section sitting around the table without me. It's very strange, and I'm missed in those scenes as well. At least I've got a good screen presence, I think. I don't even have to say anything on the screen sometimes and people are looking at me in a scene rather than Robert. I can't get into the minds of the boys this year. I think the scripts have been rushed this year, and this last one- there's no brain gags. There's no gag about it, no joke. If you're going to do it, it should have been pouring wine down, "I'm out of me skull."

Have they listened to the four of you this season?

Charles: We've all been squeezing in lines this year, more so than before. I think that's because the guys have been strapped this time. We've got some input, but there's a lot of egos involved, Rob and Doug's are bigger than anyone's.

Let's talk about your memories of 'Gunmen.'

Charles: Well, riding in on the horses was always good fun. In that episode, I got to kiss a girl, fire a gun and ride a horse; it was a complete boy's own story for me. I was kissing Loretta in the beginning in the sedan, which was good fun. It was a freezing night.

You had been lobbying for that scene for a long time.

Charles: Yeah, well it's just great to get kissed on the lips for a change. How come Rimmer could get kissed on the lips in every episode of Red Dwarf and I never got kissed on the lips? So that was quite good. I thought Lister was getting lost a bit. He needs a love interest. Come on, he's the only human being left alive three million years in the future, so Mr. Wiggly has been on bread and water for three million years, so that was quite good for that. 'Gunmen' was great. Just dressing up in the cowboy gear and riding horse- Danny was a great rider, I was completely fearless, and I've been riding a lot since then; I've gotten into it. I really enjoyed it. As we were riding through, I thought we were a bit too staid so I shouted Yee hah, and all the horses started to gallop faster. I never told anyone I did that because the others got a bit panicky and all that. It was quite scary sometimes, but the actual episode itself was great fun to make. That was my favorite episode to make, because it was such a boy's own story. It was a fantasy; you're a cowboy for a day.

How did you feel Rob and Doug letting you get kissed this season, but making you pay for it?

Charles (laughing): I kind of moaned about it a lot in the fifth series: "Chris is dead and he got laid twice! I'm alive and kicking, and I haven't been kissed in three million years!" so I kicked up a bit of a fuss about it, but Rob and Doug can be mean about that. They can be very personal in their writing, and they think we don't notice.

Was it a disappointment for when Clare Grogan came back for a single small scene in 'Psirens?'

Charles: The way she was brought back, there wasn't much of a scene, was there? We didn't even meet- she was on a monitor, and it was an illusion! I'd rather not speak about that, because I don't want to cause trouble, but it was disappointing on a number of levels. It would be nice for him to get Kochanski in the end.

But you've still got Loretta waiting in the wings.

Charles: Now that girl can kiss! And Pete Tranter's sister; I fell in love! I think that will keep him happy for a while. Next time around, I'll see if he can at least get down to his boxers.

Danny John-Jules (Cat)

Do you think your character has changed at all this time around? What's made it more interesting for you?

Danny John-Jules: My particular character? I think they've brought a bit more felinity back into the character. I think he's definitely funnier this year, better lines. I think to be honest, he did start to suffer with Kryten's progression. In being a small part anyway, his part didn't go down; it just hovered in limbo a bit. Everybody knew what I could do as the Cat, and he was just there, being solid. You always have those characters in sit-coms who are always there and they hold their end up, basically; that fourth leg on the table.

But you're content with that?

John-Jules: The thing about it in this game, as Clint Eastwood says, every man's got to know his limitations. At the same time, if you add to that what Clint should have said, he should also know how far he can go, and to get the best out of someone, you've got to ask yourself that question as well: am I giving this person the right foundations to be able to reach that point of reaching that thing where you really firing on all cylinders? You're basically talking about being complacent because I can do my part and walk out again, fine, but if you want to test me, then you'll get the best out of me.

Do you think you've been tested this time?

John-Jules: I don't know. The most I've ever been tested was in Time. I haven't been tested in Red Dwarf.

But you still get some nice bits and pieces.

John-Jules: Of course, but what Dwayne Dibbly is to me, what I would class that as I would say, that's where I would start. That would be my starting point. Anyone can learn lines. Even if they've never acted in their entire lives, they'll still be able to learn the lines; anyone can do it. What makes it special is being able to do the kind of shit that people can't do; that's what makes an actor special. No one said the best actors in the world are good at remembering lines. A kid goes to do his exams, and if you're good at remembering words, you can pass your "A" levels, because all you've got to do is revise the books they give you, and if you can remember what you read, you can pass your A levels. I haven't got an exam level to my name, but that doesn't make me stupid, so just the fact that you can learn lines doesn't help you.

Any of these guys here- Craig has got virtually a photographic memory, but that doesn't mean he's not going to forget a line on the night. I can tell you that I've got the worst memory in this cast, but on the night, anyone of those guys will tell you that I fuck up the least. That's because I work at a performance level. During the week, I can't remember the lines, but it just happens on the night. It sounds nice and fresh, and I just buzz off of the performance level of things.

Did you know when you saw the script for 'Emohawk' that this was going to be the big scene-stealer for you?

John-Jules: Yeah, I can honestly say that if Dwayne is on the telly with anybody, he's going to hold his own, because the character works, the same way the Cat works.

It's amazing how you can just stand there with the hair and teeth, do nothing, and get big laughs.

John-Jules: That's because they've never seen a black guy look like that before. We've seen pimps, we've seen the doctors; we've seen it all, but you've never seen a black nerd on television, because of the stereotyping and the way the public's been dished up black characters. They've never been given any space to say, "This is an ordinary nerdish guy," and there's one in every class in school. There's just as many black Pee Wee Hermans out there as there are white, but most people have been blinded by that stereotyping, and as a writer, you write a character that is either Eddy Murphy-ish, or the usual stuff, the Magnum sidekick, the Vietnam ex who is now flying a helicopter; wow, what a strange coincidence. But no one has ever sat there and did a normal, nerdy guy who's black, and that's why it worked, because it was original.

Why do you think he's so popular among the kids?

John-Jules: I was in the gym, and I heard two grown men talking about Dwayne Dibbly in the shower! I'm getting changed after doing a little running session in the gym, doing a little workout, and I go into the changing room, and there's two grown men, they had to be in their 30's, and they're doing "Dwayne Dibbly?" They're doing all this in the shower, not knowing that Dwayne's actually standing outside! It goes right across the board. Dwayne is harmless. He's not push anything down your throat, he doesn't want anything from anybody; he just doesn't want to be Dwayne Dibbly. People can relate to that, the kids that are bullied. There's this whole thing about bullying right now, in America and England, where kids are committing suicide because they're being bullied, they're being told that they're useless, that you're a nerd, you're a bookworm, you're this, you're that, and a lot of them are feeling depressed, and there are a lot of suicides going on.

There are so many different levels on which you can relate to Dwayne. Some people are laughing at him and saying, "Look at him. My God, he's so ugly!" I think we're all guilty of doing that at some point in our lives, where we will always say something about somebody, "Look how ugly that person is," "Look at the state of her!" We all do it, and Dwayne is the person you're talking about. Because he's come out and he's funny, he's not just another nerd who's sitting in the corner, not talking to anyone, or should I say, no one talking to him. He's there, in a situation where he's actually being a "normal" guy, or he thinks he's a normal guy. He thinks that it's great to be a nerd- I can't wait to get into my flairs and sandals; I want to get these flash clothes off me!"

Did you know last year when they were getting out all that weird clothing and putting the look together, that they were on to something?

John-Jules: The good thing about Dwayne, is it just shows you how you can spend loads of money and do the Cat- the Cat is an expensive character; it costs money to put him together, whereas Dwayne costs almost nothing, and yet he's just as popular as the Cat. You can put on an old pair of BBC trousers, a pair of sandals, some diamond socks, an anorak and a nylon shirt, and you've got a funny gag that doesn't cost you any money. Who do you think is going to be happy- the producer, right? He'll say, "My God, we're getting the same amount of feedback, and we've haven't spent any money on this character!"

The wig was from some back storeroom, the clothes were probably all 50 year-old BBC archive costumes, and the most expensive thing was the teeth. Compared to the old wardrobe- we're talking about silk, the Cat had handmade shoes, made by the people who make shoes for all the West End shows. They know my feet now, and all we have to do is order the shoes. They're expensive stuff; at least £100 a pair. I had costumes that cost thousands of pounds, but that was what the character needed.

What scene do you think really worked well in that episode?

John-Jules: When you do a character, you must know how to get the laugh, so with Dwayne, I knew how to get the laugh without even revealing my whole face. I knew they were going to laugh as soon as they saw the hair, because it's such a bizarre haircut, even though you've seen it before on Jerry Lewis and The Nutty Professor. You've seen the hair before, you've seen the buck teeth before; we've all seen this character a million times before, but you've never seen it in this situation with a black guy on television.

I knew I had to get the laugh that night, and you can ask Andy, I said, "It's best we come to the hair first," because Andy wanted me to come up and do the reveal all at once, but we ended up getting five laughs instead of one: one for the hair, one for the nose, one for the teeth, one for the touch on the teeth, because I knew that worked the first time. That's when they really went wild, was when I touched the teeth and realized...I did the same process, but I did more reveals. You do have to put your foot down sometimes, when you definitely know it's going to work. It's like the line about seersuckers and tank tops. Everyone was saying tank tops are in now, so they're not going to laugh, but when it comes to the Cat, nothing is sacred. You can do anything, and that's why I said tank tops will get a laugh from the Cat. It won't get a laugh from these guys, but it will get a laugh coming from the Cat. The audience knew the characters as well.

What did you think of the 'Gunmen' episode?

John-Jules: That was a good one. There again, it was getting to do something different and widen the scope of the character a bit, and do this Riviera Kid thing. It was a nice interlude, so I've done the Cat, I've done the Riviera Kid, I've done Dwayne; they're good characterizations, and it does tend to stretch you a bit. Now I get to play a fat slob in this one, which is all great. After they've seen you as the Cat for six years, it's still a culture shock to see them as different people. That's why it's so surprising that Dwayne was so big, because he was such an opposite.

How do you think that episode will rank up there?

John-Jules: High. I've seen some of it, and I think it will be at least in the top three. It's difficult to say, because shows are really funny. Until you actually see the series, because some of the shows that people didn't think were good, we turned around and everybody loved them. I'd like to keep my decision until the show is finished.

They used some extra music for the Riviera Kid.

John-Jules: It was my idea. I asked them to do that. What I also wanted, was just one of the times, just once, I wanted actually a guitar to be thrown into shot, and for me to catch it without looking, play it and throw it back out again. It was a time thing, but I would have liked that.

Was there anything that you would have liked to seen in this series?

John-Jules: I asked many years ago to have the thing about all the female cats. That's one thing I've been asking since series two; I think: the Cat should meet these Cat-women, and it seems to always go out the window.

How much do you want the fans to know about how close the Cat came to being written out for this series?

John-Jules: It's the truth. I don't have to lie. They all might think they don't have to tell the truth, but I can without being malicious. At the end of the day, there would be no 'Tongue Tied,' there would be no Riviera Kid, there would be no return of Dwayne Dibbly, there would be no old Cat, there would be no anything. I had to go back so they wouldn't kill off the character that I spent six years perfecting, and to be gone for a bit of money.

What really happened between seasons five and six?

John-Jules: What usually happens: we finish the series, and it was all hunky dory, and then you get a phone call saying, "We're doing Red Dwarf again." It comes through your agent, and then you say, Hey, hold on a minute. From day one, we were always told there was no "star" in Red Dwarf. That was true, except for one thing: there was only one person on star money, and everyone else was on first- time BBC money, so day one, basically, you know you've been working a bit of a sham on that level, from "there is no star of the show" to six months later, someone's getting paid several times as much as you. It's a bit of a shock to the system. But we did our gig; we were all about getting the show done.

But that's a testament that you can all work together.

John-Jules: Yeah, maybe we were just professional, and if we fought, we always came back and got the show done, and it's there in the pudding that we're together. Anyone watching that show would think that we just don't have a problem in the world, but that's through our own professionalism. If I'm not having a particularly nice time with Craig, you'd never know it on the screen, or if I'm not having a good time with any of the other guys, or if I'm having contractual problems.

So we get up to the phone call where they ask you do to season six- what made you decide now to push for a little bit more?

John-Jules: I did it before. This wasn't the first that Cat had been threatened. The first time I ever asked equality— I'm not even going to call it parity, I was told that the Cat would be re-cast in those days. That was series three, so you can make your own decisions as to who was saying what, but it wasn't a Grant Naylor Production then. So I was told that you would be recast. My reaction was the same: okay, what do I do? Pride would tell me f**k 'em, or it just gets to the point where I'm just working for money, in which case, anything I did on Red Dwarf would be just for money, so you wouldn't get the soul of the character, would you? Hence anyone would be able to play that character, which obviously wasn't the case.

So the thing is, I don't want to kill that character off. I went through this where I've never been given credit for anything for the Cat except playing it. Creativity doesn't get mentioned, and it certainly didn't show in my salary, so I've been working with a foot on my neck since day one and not only that but producing the goods. But if I wanted recognition, I would have been shouting it from the mountains all around, wouldn't I, but I was professional enough to keep what I thought to myself, and as it stands now, I'm not making waves, but what I am worried about is the fact that it's going along, and people are acting like nothing is happening. The only thing that worries me is the fact that hey, there's nothing going on here, everything is hunky dory, but that's the only worrying part about it. Then you start thinking, "Hey, I'm not going to make, and I didn't make a big deal about it. It was all done on a business level.

So the main reasons for coming back this year was to keep your character alive?

John-Jules: To keep my work alive, because I was still doing good work on Red Dwarf. I've worked without Red Dwarf. I was never out of work before I joined Red Dwarf; it's not like hey, I can't get work. I got work before. It's not a bragging thing, but when I did the first series of Red Dwarf, I was in a West End show, and the second and the fourth and the fifth, so it's not money.

Once you put the money behind you, basically you just get on with it?

John-Jules: Yeah, and even this time, I came in, I was being paid less, and then the question came up, even my professionalism as in pay- I'm no angel, but what was the biggest insult to me was even the fact that certain people thought that because I was getting paid less than the other guys, and Robert had been promoted above me, that I was going to come in with a chip on my shoulder, and walk around the studio and go through the motions and do the show, and I came in and did what they considered the best work- everyone considers it the best series ever done, and my character is definitely not slacking.

And then you get the script for 'Emohawk,' and Dwayne is back.

John-Jules: Yeah, but don't forget Rob and Doug had already started writing the series, and as it stood, I was not in the show. They started writing series six, and basically, I wasn't in the show. Negotiations had come to a standstill, and they'd said, right...I said I would do Red Dwarf as an equal, and then when it came down to it, when the news came back that Rob and Doug refused, for whatever reasons or excuse they had, that I would then make up my mind- that's it, it was all off.

Take it or leave it.

John-Jules: No, it was off. The Cat was out. They'd said that's it, we've lost him. Everyone had made up their mind that the Cat was gone. It was a phone call where Rob and I spoke on the phone. That was how the Cat was in. If I had never phoned Rob, the Cat wouldn't be in the show. I had to phone Rob, and try to get an explanation from him as to why they were doing this. If there had been a legitimate explanation, I would have understood maybe, but I always knew what it was, and everybody else knows what it is. We've been through that, and at the end of the day, it's all about money, so I said to myself, "Okay, you can be in a worse position, Danny. You could be out of work, but I said the worst thing of all is the death of the character. That would have meant me not only killing the Cat but also killing Dwayne. I would have been killing two characters now that I had put over, that I had done credit to what they had on paper.

Robert Llewellyn (Kryten)

What is it that brings you back to Red Dwarf?

Robert Llewellyn: I think it's a mixture of avaricious, single-minded greed, plus it fits in with my year It's a very contained period of time, seven weeks where I work incredibly hard, and that gives me the time and the money- particularly the time- to do what I want to do for a lot of time afterwards. I'm afraid that's a major part of the equation.

The mitigating circumstances are that I actually get on with this group. In the past, I've always got on with everyone very well, and always had a good time doing it, and it's not been a miserable experience, except for those particular days when I've got the mask on. And even on good days, like when we were in the cowboy town, I eventually got quite happy, so we've had some good recording days as well. The thing, I've realized this year is it's very easy to forget what the mask is really like, and, because it's so unpleasant, you want to forget it, so immediately as it comes off, you block it out. After a year, when I was negotiating this year's series a year later, I had completely forgotten about it. All I know is that it's bad, because I've said it's bad, but I have no memory of how it is until it goes back on the first time.

What have they done to make it different this season?

Llewellyn: It does fit better. It's not so tight around my neck. They worked out that there was some shrinkage in the foam when they cook it, so a tiny weight fluctuation on my part will really affect my neck. I didn't realize that; I always thought it was your waist! But if you eat a huge amount of food, your neck and waist increase first.

I used to have a lot of trouble with the neck being too tight last year, so it would split at the sides, so what I did this year was eat like a pig for a couple of weeks before I had the mold done, then try and lose weight before we started, and it worked; it actually fits better now. I was overweight when I went for the casting.

I heard you mention something about it getting tighter in certain areas.

Llewellyn: It has gotten better year after year, but it still does affect me. My eyes get very tired, and I think it's because I don't know what happens, but it's the combination of it being very hot so the skin around your eyes, the only part where I can lose the heat from my head, so the skin goes really weird. I don't know any way to describe it; I don't know of any other experience where that happens, and also my eyes just get tired because I can't blink so easily. The whole shading around my eyes is affected by it. Normally, if a light shines in your eyes, you're unconsciously doing something to shield yourself, but when I've got that head on, it affects my vision so that I don't know where the bloody lights are coming from, and it really hurts. That's the thing that's always been the biggest problem. From that point of view this year, the physical side effects are the minimum that I've ever had; they've been very very-low.

Did you make any lobbying effort to use the American mask this year?

Robert: I did, but they wouldn't have it. The thing is, I don't know what would have happened if I said, "If I don't have the American mask, I won't do the show!" They were certainly prepared to push me to the very limit, because I was adamant about it for a long time, two to three months, absolutely saying, "I won't do it without the American mask!" and gradually they out-lasted me. I should have stood up for it more.

They also made your costume a little more comfortable this year, didn't they?

Llewellyn: It was a huge improvement. I think it looks better too. I much prefer the look of it, and I can sit down in it, and it's much less hot. That's made the process a lot less painful.

What was it like in previous years?

Llewellyn: It was very heavy and hot. It actually weighed a lot so it was an effort to stand up in it. It was also very tight, so I couldn't sit down. It was about three layers thick, so it was like wearing a really thick, quilted boiler suit on a very hot stage, with a plastic bag over your head. When I take this one off, the undershirt I wear is soaked, but not so soaked that I can wring it out. Honestly, I used to stand in the dressing room and I could twist my shirt and it would be would be sodden with sweat.

Now that we've gotten a lot of the negative things out of the way, what were some of the positive aspects of working on this series?

Llewellyn: There's that really lovely feeling where you've been rehearsing it and even if the crew laughs a bit during rehearsal, when you actually do it on the night and the audience explodes with a huge roar of laughter, and then you feel as if the thing has suddenly come together. You do feel like a team, and part of a bigger thing. I love that. It's an odd experience, because in everything else I do that's live performing, there's an audience there, and as a performer, I'm super-aware of the audience. On this show, it's taken me a long time to get used to the fact that I'm really not aware of them at all. The only time I'm aware is in-between scenes. It's very odd, because I'm much more removed from it.

They've put you in a few strange situations again this year, starting with the cube Kryten from the episode one.

Llewellyn: This show does prepare you for anything. Every other show is so mundane to work on, because this is so bizarre. Yeah, in the first week on this, I was in a power station, squashed into a small polystyrene box. I had to walk along a corrugated steel floor with shoes that didn't slip and fall on my face. They're the most incredible scrapes that we get into, the most incredible combination of events.

How did you like doing 'Gunmen of the Apocalypse?'

Llewellyn: It was great fun to get out and ride horses and shoot proper guns with the cowboys. It was good fun. We'd never done that, and it was like boy's day out. It was an extraordinary adventure. The negative side is that I had to get up so bloody early; I was in the mask at 5:30 in the morning. But it was fun, and the guys that we worked with, the horse/stunt guys were brilliant.

There was some scary stuff, such as being wired up for the gunshots.

Llewellyn: Yeah, but I've done it enough times to know that they're very safety conscious. I've had one very slight injury being shocked once. I usually get shot at least twice a series, so it's become quite commonplace.

Some of the sequences with you as the drunken sheriff were quite funny.

Llewellyn: It was such a mad idea that there was this robot who was a drunken sheriff in a cowboy town. Whatever you did with it was going to be funny.

The scene where you're struck by the sign got big laughs.

Robert: It was such a fluke. That sort of thing is amazing, because I've done those sorts of equivalent gags in, and trying to get it to work, you do it 50 times, and that was just a pure fluke; it's never happened before where we only took one take of that. We never did another take of it. I had no idea what was going to happen. I didn't know if the sign would come down, I didn't know where I'd be when it came down, we never ever rehearsed it had we, we never even tried it, so luck was on our side there.

The one that never worked out was the one with the doves.

Llewellyn: When you go back to start describing why you're in a muddy field, throwing a couple of doves with no wings in the air; then it gets complicated. Kryten's artificial reality inside his brain, which the rest of the crew has broken into, Kryten is in this cowboy town, playing the sheriff, and he's trying to find a dove program, which is a peace-spreading computer virus, which will defeat the virus that is spreading through Starbug's navigation system- that's pretty good! I've done well so far.

So right at the end of the sequence, in the artificial reality, Kryten draws his guns on the bad viruses, who are wicked, evil cowboys. The guns turn into doves, which fly away- that's the theory, so I was standing in a muddy field, with a couple of doves, one in each hand; lovely white doves, and I had to look like I was drawing my guns, and then these two doves were going to fly off into the heavens, and it was going to be rather dramatic, rather like the last shots of Blade Runner, so I was given the two doves, and I picked them up, and went to draw the guns, and threw them in the air, and they dropped on the floor, because they'd had their wings clipped, so they wouldn't fly away, so they were non-flying, flying doves, so they said "Throw them harder!" so we looked around for the RSPCA, and they weren't there, so I threw them as hard as I could, and they went up about four feet, and they fell flat down on the ground, so that was really about it. That day was really funny altogether.

You and Craig seemed to have a lot of fun with the gangster sequence.

Llewellyn: The thing with Kryten is, the combination of the mask and the costume has always been a tough gig, like when I played Jake Bullet, the mask was bad, but at least I had a nice suit on, and I feel extra comfortable, because I'm used to being uncomfortable that having one of those discomforts taken away is a real joy. I can sit down and cross my legs and I've got my hands free, and I'm not boiling hot- it's bliss to be in normal clothes. It was the same with the gangster. It was a really beautiful suit, and a lovely big coat. It was a very cold night, but I was warm on location that night.

What was the most uncomfortable part?

Llewellyn: The makeup bus in the morning. It was a particularly bad time, because the bus was wobbly, so whenever anyone came in, or left, I got a glue brush up my nose or in my ear or my eye. It got a little bit tight that day. I had to have a walk in the field and kick a log to calm down. It was a tough day, but it was fun. Once it was going, I really enjoyed myself that day.

And the funniest thing?

Llewellyn: When we were all on the horses for the ride at the end of the day. What was funny about it was that it typified the four of us. It distilled the essence of our four characters at that moment, because I've ridden horses a lot and I've fallen off them a lot, so I have a lot of experience with that and therefore fear. Chris hadn't ridden them a lot, but is a sensible human being, and therefore was also scared. Danny had ridden a little bit, and was actually very good and wasn't scared.

Craig had never ridden a horse before in his life, but has no fear, therefore is extremely dangerous. He kept saying, 'Giddiup!' and these horses were very frisky and were capable of attaining incredible speeds, as I soon discovered in the back field.

Have you found that you're getting more and more expository lines this season?

Llewellyn: They've tried to spread them a bit more this year. Craig's done a lot more this year than he did last year, so we've shared them a bit more. Certainly my character's job is to explain why the psi-scan is reading whatever it is, the incredibly complex explanation, an extremely deep and difficult theory about time and space. They're very hard lines to learn. I'm now really quite good at learning lines whereas a few years ago I was terrible at it. It's just forced me to learn ways to do it. The thing is that I spend sometimes 4 or 5 hours, usually on the Tuesday night of each week at home just walking up and down saying them again and again and again. I might say one difficult speech 40 or 50 times, literally that many times until my voice starts to go hoarse, but I'd wake up on Wednesday morning and I'm relaxed, because I think at least I know that, and it just comes out. It is that kind of effort that's required, and I forget that before I start, that it's not just the time in rehearsals that I put into the shows, and we all do. I know Chris does. Craig is very lucky. He's got a very quick memory, and he picks up lines very fast. Danny has the annoying ability of not being able to do them once in rehearsals and then being perfect on the night, but Chris and I both have to do a lot of work behind the scenes to get them right.

What do you think the highlight of this series was for you?

Llewellyn: I honestly think I can't tell until I see it. Whenever I see the show, I'm amazed at what it looks like. When I saw last year's show in broadcast, which was the first time I'd ever seen them- especially when they're joined in with the model shots which we never see, and the sound's been done, I just think it's a really good show, and I feel by then that... because I don't see myself, it's a really weird experience. I can't bear watching myself in other things; when I'm on the screen in other programs, I don't watch them, but this I really enjoy watching. Obviously I'm remembering when we were recording it, and I can remember the things that went wrong that have now been cut out very carefully, but on the whole, I go with the story. I'm completely swept along with it, so I've actually become a real fan of Red Dwarf apart from- it has nothing to do with being in it. It doesn't make any sense, but it really is like a separate experience seeing it.

I know everyone complains at the end of the year, and says they'll never do it again, but could you see yourself come back for a seventh season?

Robert: I'm always torn, but yes, there definitely is. The series could run and run, and I think this is the funniest series yet. I think they're brilliant writers. It's not easy writing to do, and I curse them nightly because the lines are so bloody difficult to do, but they're so good, and they've very funny, and they come up with amazingly un-clichéd, refreshingly new humor.

There are some aspects of it I'm not wild about; I'm not a big scatological poo joke fan, but it works. I throw in poo jokes in my own stand-up stuff, because you can get big cheap laughs, but I love it when they get something slightly more whacky or something different. Their character observation is brilliant. It's uncanny. Their development of our four characters is so... it gets closer and closer to the people we are underneath, which is a bit disturbing. With Chris, you're a bloody git, or with Craig you're an utter slob, or with Dan you're completely vain, or with me, you're a robot who loves washing up. I love washing up. How did they know before they met me? I'd rather wash up than sit around chatting after a meal. That's what I normally do.

Has there been any talk to you about a film?

Llewellyn: They've asked me if that happens if I would. I would, I'd love to do a movie; I might even put up with the makeup. My opinion is that I just want Kryten's head to get blown up and to get a new head, and then I'll do it at the drop of a hat. I love doing the series. I love working with the other guys. I just feel I'm getting on a bit now, and it's so tiring and so mentally debilitating that I've really had enough, and I think Rob and Doug know that this year.

So every year they have to up the ante a little bit to get you back?

Llewellyn: Well yeah, but I'm always convinced that they'll never do another series. Last year, I was utterly convinced that was it, they've done five years; there's no way they'd ever do another one. I was completely sure; that's why I didn't even think about it, especially because we were going to America. It just seemed like, well, there's no way we'll ever do that again!

What do you remember the funniest thing that happened to you this seas?

Llewellyn: On that particular day, it was the horses. When we were all on the horses for the ride at the end of the day, what was funny about it was that it typified the four of us. It distilled the essence of our four characters at that moment, because I've ridden horses a lot and I've fallen off them a lot, so I have a lot of experience with that and therefore fear. Chris hadn't ridden them a lot, but is a sensible human being, and therefore was also scared. Danny had ridden a little bit, and was actually very good and wasn't scared. Craig had never ridden a horse before in his life, but has no fear, therefore is extremely dangerous. He kept saying, giddiup, and these horses were very frisky and were capable of attaining incredible speeds, as I soon discovered in the back field.

Rob Grant/Doug Naylor (Writer/Co-Creators)

What was the motivation for doing season six in the way it's being done now?

Doug Naylor: It was to take it in a different direction and to give it a new energy. We felt if they were forced into a much smaller craft with low supplies, it would give a whole new, fresh feel to the series. Obviously you don't know if it's going to work or not in advance, but we had to make a decision quite early on to say, 'Okay, Red Dwarf is out!' To that extent, it has given it a different feel. Whether it's better or not, I don't know, but it's certainly different from the other series.

Rob Grant: We also felt that in series five that it was more exciting when we were in Starbug, where they were more hands-on and in control. They could run away from things, they could be fired at in a way that you can't really do with an enormous ship.

Naylor: It was really back to basics. It's recession Dwarf, really.

Grant: And they're under more privation, and they're having to suffer more. We always try and move the characters along every season, and we felt- and it was reflected in the fan opinion we were getting- that we were under-using Holly and the Cat. We thought that by getting rid of one of them, at least temporarily, the function of the remaining character would be enhanced, and I feel that has worked. The balance has been split more evenly in the sixth series.

Naylor: Danny has also got far more of a role. I don't quite agree with Rob that it was a choice of either/or. Holly had to go because Holly was on board Red Dwarf, but Danny having more of a role gave us a whole extra energy.

Grant: Holly's energy has kind of been split between the Cat and Kryten, really.

What about Rimmer, where you changed something fundamental to his character, which was his being a hologram?

Naylor: Again, it gave him a whole new dimension, a whole new area to put the character into.

Grant: When we made the decision in 'Legion' to give him a hard light drive, it was a function of the plot. We originally intended to go back to the status quo at the end of the show, but then we thought, why? It's a nice idea that we've got the option of the hard light drive when we needed it, so we kept it in and it stayed.

Naylor: Also, because the history of the series has been that the BBC has always commissioned the series incredibly late for whatever reasons. With most series, you generally get at least a year's notice, but we've generally had from three to four months, and then been told we have to deliver on a certain day. This year was even crazier even by the crazy standards of Red Dwarf. There was a whole commotion about changing the format, and changing certain characters, which we resisted.

Changing them in what way?

Naylor: Changing them in not having necessarily the lineup we wanted, which we resisted, but that resulted in an even greater delay in the commissioning process. For the first three or four months, it was back to our bachelor days for Rob and I, trying to write a series with so little time.

Do you think some of the stories have suffered, either by not being polished enough, or little bits and pieces getting by you that wouldn't have gotten by if you had more time?

Naylor: I can't say yes or no at the moment until we get into the edit. Certainly in the past, we've changed stories in the edit. 'Dimension Jump' for example, was changed quite substantially in the edit; a whole new ending was put on. What did you have in mind specifically?

Like putting a reference to Red Dwarf at the end of episode six.

Naylor: There's always been that situation of things slipping by, and so you have to stay on your feet. That happens constantly. That's why we're in and out of the scanner talking to Andy, changing lines and changing shots. That's why we have re-shoot days.

What made you decide on Andy and Justin as the director and producer?

Naylor: Justin was recommended to us by Gilly [Archer]. We had never worked with him before, but then we worked with him on The 10%ers. Andy was again recommended by Gilly. We wanted to have Steve Bendelack, who we knew from our old Spitting Image days, but ultimately he wasn't able to do it, and Gilly said, 'Why don't you meet with Andy; I'm sure you'll get along really well with him,' so apart from The 10%ers, we were working with two people we didn't really know that well, but for such a tough series, to be thrown in with two people we didn't know, it worked out very well.

Didn't you previously talk about maybe directing this series yourselves?

Naylor: We were keen to do that, but because of the commissioning process, that was completely nailed on the head immediately.

As you went into production, is it true that the only script that was ready was 'Psirens?'

Naylor: No, three were written when we went into the series. We had two on the boil, but 'Parasites' was one we were going to do, but it just fell away. There was another one about meeting people who edit all pain out of their lives; that was a really good idea, but it never really took off.

What was 'Parasites' about?

Grant: It may emerge again, so we'd better not talk about it.

So it hasn't disappeared entirely.

Grant: They never do; they never disappear. There are ideas in this series that go right back to the first season.

Naylor: 'Unreality Minefield' is about three years old.'

With 'Psirens,' it almost felt as though you were going for an Aliens-type feel at times.

Naylor: The whole series has got a kind of Jason and the Argonauts feel. 'Psirens' is obviously very much that genre, and I think the whole series has that feel to it.

What was the thinking about bringing in so many big guest stars in that episode, as well as Clare Grogan who makes her long-awaited return?

Naylor: That was a difficult day- the first couple of days of shooting are always difficult, because nobody's up to speed, but when it was all put together, I thought it was fine.

Grant: I think Kochanski is better as an icon than she would be hanging around. We had to decide right from the start if we were going to take this kind of serial idea through it, which this show was, and really is nice to get a few column inches in the newspapers through guest cameos. We do that every season. And with things like Kryten's creator, when we got the idea for this series, we had wanted to bring in Kryten's creator, so we thought it would be nice to get in someone good.

Naylor: Jenny Agutter had expressed an interest. She actually contacted us and said, "I'd love to appear!' so that's why Jenny Agutter was in it. With the guitar solo that Phil Manzanera does, our original idea was to approach Brian May from Queen. We thought, why don't we ask both of them [May and his wife, Dobson] and he couldn't do it because he was going on tour, but Anita said yes.

Grant: She did it as a bit of fun, really. If we hadn't been so snowed under by the script, we might have been tried to do something more with it.

How do you feel the episode turned out?

Naylor: We can't say until it's edited.

Grant: I do think that Jenny and Anita were great. I was just sorry that they weren't in bigger parts, that they were just cameos.

Naylor: There's such a change in the episodes when they're edited. You take five minutes out of a show, because they're all 34 minutes, so they do change. You get the model shots, and you take out some of the stuff that doesn't work; I'm convinced that you can improve any show by 15-20 percent with a good edit.

With 'Legion,' it feels like the success or failure of the episode was going to depend largely on the ending, which must have been a worrying proposition.

Grant: Yes, that's always a nightmare.

Naylor: But you're saying that because at the moment it looks so bad, but yes, that's not a new situation. Quite a large percentage of our special FX budget has gone into making that shot work, but they seem confident that they can do it.

Grant: With the banquet scene, we're quite confident that all the elements are there; I don't think that's so much a mystery as whether or not the Legion effect will work.

Grant: At the time, we really weren't in a position to worry about that.

Naylor: The morphing was out of our control; not so much the banquet scene. With the morphing sequence, no one really knew how to do it, and there were a lot oh different attempts. I don't think we're the best person to ask about the morphing sequence, because having seen it so many times, you need somebody fresh to watch it. Having said that, I think the start of 'Legion,' the first seven minutes, is the funniest of the series, the space weevil and the red alert bulb.

The thing is, it's so totally unimportant what we think, and what we think changes. That's why we're always interested in what is a favorite episode. Ultimately you can't write it if you don't believe it, but of course you're greatly influenced by what is perceived as working.

What was the thought about doing another Rimmer-centric episode with **'**Rimmerworld?**'**

Grant: I think it's less so than say, Ace was, and in fact Chris is out of it as much as he is in it. It is about Rimmerworld, but he doesn't make an appearance there until the last scene in 'Rimmerworld,' so it's more about all of them, really.

Naylor: The thing about 'Terrorform' is that he's not in the first ten minutes at all, but people say, "Oh, that's a Rimmer story!" He's at the heart of the action which has been caused by something he's done, but if he's not there, does that count as his story?

Grant: We tried to pretty much make that the order of the day for this series, overall, that everyone has their say. In 'Emohawk,' they all have their set pieces.

Everyone seems to think that **'**Gunmen**'** is going to be the big episode of this series.

Grant: If you look at the assemblies, 'Legion' is very strong, and we've re-shot the Star Drive sequence at the end of that.

Naylor: And when you look at 'Emohawk' as well, but yes, I think 'Gunmen' will be a good show.

Grant: It's actually the shortest show so far.

Naylor: But that's because it's been edited so tightly, whereas the other assemblies haven't been. It makes a hell of a difference when you're watching a tighter assembly. I think that as a piece of production, it's a splendidly produced piece of work.

Did you spend a lot of time watching old westerns to get a feel for them?

Naylor: That's true, but getting to watch a lot of great westerns; that's not very tough, but in terms of actually spending actual writing time...

Grant: We were very conscious of having to avoid 'Shadow of the Gun.'

Naylor: It was very difficult, because we had to satisfy ourselves that this location existed before we wrote the script. It would have just been a disaster to have written a script that was ultimately too ambitious and we couldn't use.

What do you think the strongest sequence in 'Gunmen?'

Grant: I think it's when the guys come into town. Everyone excelled; I think the model work was excellent.

Naylor: Graham did a terrific job as editor, doing the blue matte stuff. The model shots have really improved because of that.

Were you originally going to give the Jennifer Calvert character a bit more in this series?

Grant: That was the thought, to give Lister a romance with a computer sprite. At one time, we were talking about getting her out into the ship, and we thought it would be interesting to mix it up, having this completely amoral person, but then we thought it would cut against Rimmer, so we didn't do it.

Did you work around the amount of material that could be shot in Laredo after seeing it and what could be done?

Naylor: We said to Andy, "Go find a Western town, because we want to write a cowboy one, and tell us if there are any." He went to several places and said, "The best one is Laredo, and it's great!" It was actually going to be shot at night, until we realized what a logistical nightmare that would be, because it was outside London, so we would need overnights; all those things, so it had to be changed to the day. Shooting on video in England during the day always looks horrible, but we were absolutely dead lucky that we had such a great day.

Was 'Emohawk' meant to be the big crowd pleaser?

Grant: We wanted to do a sequel to 'Polymorph, and also bring Duane back. In fact, at one point, we were going to bring Duane back as the Cat's alter ego, and at times of stress he would become Duane, but we found it got in the way of the story, but we were desperate to bring Duane back, and it fit so well to bring back Ace and Duane at the same time, because they're variants of the main characters.

Naylor: But again, that's even less than the main half of the story. The middle is the wedding sequence with Lister and the beginning of that, which we regret we cut down, was quite a long scene in the cockpit.

With the final episode, I'm a little confused. As producers, you know there's not much time and money left, and yet as the writers you still want to do an interesting story. Is there a point beyond which you can't push your creative people any more with the resources they have?

Grant: What we always do with these things-

Naylor: Is that true? It's not that easy, but we'll get through it.

Grant: What we do is write a script, and we usually notify the departments who are going to have trouble with it and ask them if it's going to be a problem before it gets into the scripts, so we said to both makeup and costume, "Do you have a problem with their future selves, and making them fat and debauched?" and everybody said no.

Naylor: I have a feeling you might be right today, Joe, if it falls apart; you might be right.

But at that point, you know it's do-able.

Naylor: Oh yes, there's a constant thing throughout the series: is it possible to do this, have we got- it's like the Western. It's no good writing a Western and then not knowing there is one, because it would just look awful.

Grant: I think the biggest challenge to the crew this time around was 'Emohawk,' because Effects had to built the Emohawk, Andy had a lot of effects to do, and Mel had a very short time to build his set, and makeup and wardrobe had no time at all to get the GELFs together, but they did a miraculous job.

Were you aware of how Craig was going to feel about being a brain in a jar?

Naylor: No, you always write the funniest script and totally ignore egos, but having said that, when you say 'not for the eyes of the cast,' that might be because you want to go through the script, and if someone's part is weak, you might try and improve that part, and fix it before the table reading.

Grant: You always do the good story.

Naylor: Absolutely. In that case, Craig actually said that he was wrong and he overreacted, and he was tired, and all those things.

How do you think this episode is turning out as a season-ending story?

Grant: It's not necessarily going to be the last show transmitted.

Naylor: I think it's going to be quite a good one. Certainly with all the deaths at the end, you're going to think, "Oh, they're all going to go!"

It's probably too early to ask, but how much potential do you think this season has as opposed to the previous five?

Grant: I think it's better. With every series we've done so far, I thought has been better than the previous one, and if it's not, we're doing something wrong.

Andy DeEmmony (Director)

How did you come to do Red Dwarf?

Andy DeEmmony: I heard they were looking for a director, and sent them my show reel. We had a couple of meetings and then I fell for it! (laughing)

Was it difficult, getting used to having the two writer/producers there while you're directing?

DeEmmony: A lot, actually, but I had certain warnings that I knew we'd be going through that. To fight wouldn't have been productive anyway; as it is, after the first couple I got their trust a bit so they're here far less, and leave a lot more to me. I wanted to get a handle on what they're aiming at, which I now feel I have, so we're working in the same direction towards the same end.

I suppose the hardest handle to get onto was between reality and slapstick. The temptation for me visually is if you can see a bit of business that can get a laugh as well, you go for it to try and increase the density of the laughs. I often find the problem with this is there are so many laughs, it starts getting in the way of everything else. Your pacing can't be there, because it's gag, another line; gag, another line constantly throughout the show, so it gets a little difficult at times to tell a story or build any pace or excitement. I'm having to steer myself away from some of the more visual jokes unless they can be very real, so everything has to be very believable, very straight, nothing played for the laugh but instead played a little low, and then ride the jokes off it, rather than asking for them, which I think is the right way to do it here.

What sort of problems did you run into during the filming of Psirens those first few weeks?

DeEmmony: I think everybody was very cold in terms of starting on the series. Everyone is in the flow now and it's much easier, but then they were a bit sluggish about getting into the swing of things.

How long did it take you to start clicking with the cast?

DeEmmony: Not very long, actually. I thought that would be far more of a problem, but they seemed quite happy to give me what I needed. Everybody was really tired, because we were working long hours, and things could get a bit touchy, but they were all very good.

Tell me about some of the guest stars you've brought in for this series.

DeEmmony: Some of the guest artists have been very good: Jenny Agutter, Richard Ridings, who was excellent, doing his whole monologue while eating a beef burger! He took a great big chunk out of it and then did his speech.

I thought it was funny, watching you coach Claire Grogan in the difference between 'Sta-sis' and 'Stay-sis.'

DeEmmony: In fairness, she got really nervous in going straight after Anita Dobson. She didn't want to do it after that, and in the end, we got all the material we needed, but it was very difficult. I could never see the match between the character she plays and the sort of character Craig is; you'd need some bitch queen from hell to settle him. We had Jennifer Calvert in one episode, who was brilliant. Again, it's that believability factor. Some people see comedy, and want to play it for laughs, pull a few funny faces, and try to get the laughs, and some people play it straight. I think she did an excellent job. Denis Lill was great as Death.

Did you find that some of the scenes shot late in the day are coming back to haunt you now? It seemed like you had to shoot them too little too late.

DeEmmony: Yeah, they're the re-shoot bits we are picking up at the end; three or four scenes, I'm more than happy about re-shooting them for exactly that reason: we banged them out. It's very odd when you think we're doing a sitcom, but the effects and everything else involved with what you're doing are so phenomenal.

One of the amazing things about this show is the amount of stuff that has to be done on the floor, such as split screen and so forth. It must be difficult to concentrate on the performances when you're more conscious of where a person is standing.

DeEmmony: What you really want to do is to grill everyone in rehearsal so everyone is very slick. With the splits in 'Psirens' with the two Listers, we got the three or four passes or whatever and it cut together fine. With the final episode, we talked it through a couple of times and roughly blocked it, but by doing the pickups on Friday, we lost a day of rehearsal, which definitely slowed it down.

The thing with the splits is, Ed did the big wide with the split, does the other side, and then picks up with individual shots. I prefer to go for the line cut, where all my shots are done around two or three line cuts and then we put them together. I've been proved wrong, because we very rarely get any kind of line cuts. If we get past three or four lines together, I'm doing well, so we end up with a laborious process, but I'd rather at least aim to do it multi-camera, and pull back to a single camera than not.

I must admit I'm not a fan of splits. I think one of the reasons I got this gig is because my shows had lots of different effects and cheats on them, but you have to make them so fleeting and minimal that you're not pushing it. Things like today, I'm trying to create odd splits, rather than leaving a big gap down the middle so we've got something in a quarter of the frame, rather than a line down the middle.

I notice you also do story boards on a lot of your scenes.

DeEmmony: By now, I haven't got time to storyboard anything. When we did the Laredo western shoot, I had rough storyboards for that, just so I could tick off frames. The big difficulty was jumping out of sequence, so to get through everything in a day there, when I've got a camera in one position, I wanted to do the shots from that position, so we tried to shoot shots from other scenes and any other scenes out of sequence, so I had to tick off the boxes and say, "I've got the scene that connect this, this, and this,' and hopefully that made it quicker.

A lot of people seem to think the Laredo episode was the best of the six in terms of the humor, the style, and the expansiveness of the story. Have you found that to be true as well, or do you have a different favorite?

DeEmmony: I would say the Laredo one, certainly. I haven't seen the assembly yet for 'Emohawk,' and things like 'Psirens' and 'Legion' to a certain extent, so much will happen in the post-production, but those four out of the six I would say- probably 'Legion' not quite as much. Laredo's got to be big, just because we've got so much; it was almost a feature film storyline and we didn't get lost in exposition, where Robert as Kryten sometimes ends up as almost an exposition machine, and he has so much trouble with his lines. It's maddening to keep the gags in with it, and not let a flat area where you could lose people who might switch off.

Tell me about some of the shots you're re-doing on Friday.

DeEmmony: We're re-doing a compactor scene with Robert in the box. At the last minute, we were doing the shot where he walks away from camera to the edge and looks down. We now have him walking to camera which is funnier. I want to do a shot where he's walking towards camera, laugh, and then we do an out of camera shot, as he's walking away to the edge.

With the Temptresses, I'm more than pleased to be doing that one again, because I didn't want to do it like that in the first place. I think the argument is it's being played for Danny's benefit, and since the Cat isn't too bright, it wouldn't be too subtle, so we're going to try and make it look much vampire and beef that up a little bit. We're also re-doing the star drive scene. Rob and Doug don't like the actual machine we've got, so we're changing the machine.

As well as the crew hanging in space.

DeEmmony: I think the other scene would work when it has the wind and the sound on it, but we're not doing a hanging scene this time. We're doing a gripping shot and we'll blow a lot of stuff past them on the wind machine. We also had a continuity problem with Chris, who should have been in blue, but I don't think at that stage, we'd really got our head around it, because were working on the first script, and then got the script for Legion' and jumped into that scene, and nothing else from 'Legion' was done at that time; just that scene, and Chris was in red not blue, so we're re-doing that one. I feel sorry for Robert, who's not really keen on another mask, but he'll be out in three days, so he's got to look at it that way.

What is it you've done this series that you're proudest of?

DeEmmony: They just love giving me a script and saying, "See if you can do that!" as a little test each time. A lot of the Western stuff, the saloon scenes with the fights and the knife-throwing, and trying to figure out how Danny actually shoots two bullets out of the air and get a laugh, which we actually managed to do. The bullwhip was the hardest one to do actually. It worked, but it still looks a bit like a fishing rod.

The scene with Rimmer kissing the female Rimmer. I like very much when we mange to do it in camera. We did have the glass and the blue screen ready, and we were going to try and kiss the same spot on the glass, but very few effects shots like that work, especially with a kiss.

I like the dock scenes, with the black and white which I'm a big fan of. I liked the model shot in 'Psirens' in the quarry with the big Starbug. I liked the turntable shot as well, with Lister kissing the monster. When that's finished, I think it's going to be quite fun. And I liked some of the scenes we just shot in 'Emohawk.'

Which were quite difficult, especially with the rubber monster hitting the floor.

DeEmmony: That's another thing I'm not used to: not seeing things until the day of the shoot. It's very hard, because you've camera-scripted it in your mind, and then you're given things that are not necessarily bad but different from the way you'd seen it, which throws you completely. When we get to the Emohawk, it worked fine in the end, but it was nothing like I'd imagined. I imagined a bird sort of thing, but it looked more like a sexual aid! It worked in the end, they all struggle through.

I really liked the throne room scene in 'Rimmerworld.' If it's a climactic effect, you try to spend a little more time on it, and I quite liked the different pace. It will probably be much tighter and shorter in the end, but trying to show a different environment, a different world and different characterizations of the different Rimmers; it was quite nice to do that.

stuff on the talkback, so there's a lot of effects on the Thursday, so you want to be in the thick of it. I normally direct from the floor anyway. I prefer it, even if it's multi-camera, certain vision mixers from Spitting Image would let me cut from the floor, so I can sit and watch the monitor here, and give them their cues.

It's very difficult- I know a lot of people like to give actors complete marks, lines, head turn points; I much prefer watching rehearsals and talking about performances and letting it play, and then camera scripting it to them, rather than trying to pin them down, and I'd much rather change shots than change the performance and lose the realism.

Are you fairly comfortable as the director if one of the actors tells you he's not happy about a line that his character might not say?

DeEmmony: Yes, they know a lot of things that are historical as well. Getting my head around the fact that Chris could never touch anything threw me a bit at first. There were other technical character points as well. I wouldn't hold them down to how I saw the characters; I would lean on my interpretation as being the size of the performance, the pace, so that the whole piece works together. They've got the characters down very well, and I can accept that and not push them in a particular direction they don't want to go# and they know how to ad lib for their characters as well.

Mel Bibby (Production Designer)

When does most of the designing get done- is it on the fly?

Mel Bibby: At this moment in time, yes. We got the scripts the second week in January so it was about four weeks. We had about a week to design the whole concept of the thing, and three weeks to build it. That's quite a big build for us.

So that didn't leave much time for the extra stuff for the first episode.

Bibby: We knew about the compactor about three or four weeks ahead, so that was a real luxury. We didn't know where we were going to do it, which is why we made the compactor totally mobile.

It's all sectioned so you can strip it down and move it around. One of the requirements for that was it should be able to go down a narrow staircase in a power station in sections and then rebuilt anywhere.

Did you go out and see any of the locations in advance?

Bibby: Yeah, we came down on the initial recces [location scouts] and measured the staircase and such.

I was thinking about the Marco Polo Building for 'Legion.'

Bibby: We went on a pre-recce of that. The thing about this program is...on a lot of jobs, we're not getting a choice of locations are we? On a lot of jobs, we obviously say it will work for some aspects and not work on others, can we find alternatives? We haven't had the time, nor has Suzanne the location manager, to really go out and find an alternative, so we had to go with what's available.

What was particularly challenging on this series from the design standpoint?

Bibby: I think the only difference this year has been to try for a two-tier situation, although we haven't actually used the two tiers as yet. That was the only challenging bit: to actually get a staircase and a gantry and everything else, and also to get lights above it.

With the cockpit, where it's lit from beneath, is that the way John Pomphrey wanted it, or is it the same as last year?

Bibby: It's always been the same. If you go back to the original scripts, it said the first time we saw Starbug, they stepped down from the cockpit into the mid-section, which meant it needed a raised floor. It was my decision to put a mesh floor in, so John Pomphrey could light through it. Had it been a solid floor, you wouldn't have been able to light it, but with a mesh floor, John brought the lights in, and we thought, 'Oh, that looks nice!'

This isn't the first time you've all the monitors to pipe in the video signals, has it?

Bibby: No, in the science lab, we used to have several monitors, but once we got rid of the science lab, it released monitors, which are hired in, and they'd like to keep it down to the same budget costs per year, so if you have nine monitors on the first series, you end up with nine monitors on the sixth, because the budgets the same.

You also had computers in the Starbug cockpit?

Bibby: The navi-comps, yeah. They're a piece of navigational systems, where you can actually punch in where you are and you can see them working. They're actually programmed with a map of Europe, so we tend to zoom in on the Greek Islands, which looks like an asteroid belt. They're made for small yachts and small boats, and actually plots the coast of Europe. It's on a little cartridge that plugs into the navi-comp. It gives off a very good green glow, and from our point of view, they look like asteroid belts. They're actually on loan from the company to us, because we're actually showing them on screen. You've got to give Springer the prop buyer credit for them, because I didn't know they existed until he found them and brought them in.

Was there always been four stations for the characters to sit?

Bibby: Prior to this, the cockpit was smaller, but we expanded it this year simply because they wanted to seat Rimmer and they wanted to seat Kryten in the back. Prior to that, they would just stand up. They got over the problem with Chris because of the hard light drive. In the first episode, he was soft light, and used to sit, but he could only talk into the mike. Now, when he's hard light, he can touch things.

You rationalized these upgrades by saying they had been scavenging?

Bibby: I once said that Steve and I used to root through skips to find a set, and that was kind of misused in the sense that we've looked through skips to find sets for every situation; we don't. That was a one-off occasion in 'DNA,' where there just happened to be a commercial going on next door. They were using a lot of polystyrene and we went in to see them, and the prop master knew the art director, and we said, 'Can we have your polystyrene when you're finished with it?' He said, 'Yes, we'll throw it in the skip and you can get it out,' and that was that.

What sort of new features did you include in the galley?

Bibby: Absolutely none. The recycling unit was scripted. Andy the director thought it might be rather nice to actually use a fruit dispenser, and we originally had oranges floating on top of it, but they were subsequently dismissed, and we put all sorts of crap in it, but yes, a lot of action takes place there.

And the medical unit gets re-dressed?

Bibby: It takes the place of the old science lab, which used to be a medical/ science unit. Again, had we had the full scripts up front, I think we could have done a better job on that, because we didn't know what the action was going to be. We just had to build a room with a bed coming out, and suddenly we started putting all this other stuff in.

The beds were also built into it for the first episode as well?

Bibby: That was all rigged off the gantry with a counterweight balance system. It was the only script we had at the time, so we designed it for that particular episode, and all the subsequent stuff that went on like the medi-bed, and the AR was news to us. I think I would have done a lot more with that room if I had known there was going to be that much action in it. I would have made it more interesting for a start shape-wise, and a bit bigger. I don't think you worry about where things came from. I would have given it more depth up front, but when you don't have the script, you don't know what's going to come.

One of the nice sets in 'Legion' was Lister's bedroom for Legion. I thought you swiped the jukebox from the Noel Gay office.

Bibby: We thought about it, but the insurance risk value would be too much. You may as well go to a hire company and pick it up from them. We did think about going into Noel Gay and nicking theirs- it would have been a good wheeze, but Steve backed out at the last minute!

So you were coming up with ideas for what would make Lister happy.

Bibby: That's right. It was somewhat difficult, because we could never actually get a community decision as to what it should really look like. It was always Legion's tastes, but with Lister's mind, so therefore we went straight down the middle and kept it in good taste, but with Lister's requirements, such as a jukebox and some naff rock and roll neon signs. It was still in good taste to a certain extent, because Legion created it. That was difficult, actually; we could have gone over the top with it, and made it a pure slum, to go with Lister's character- leopard skin wallpaper, but we decided to go the other way.

I noticed there weren't any sleeping quarters this season.

Bibby: There haven't been any waking up or sleeping scenes at all.

What were you trying to do with the re-dressed escape pod?

Bibby: That was designed for a one-off script where it was just Rimmer in a seat, standing up and firing the flares and then the other script came in and we thought, 'We can use this for another script!' I think it looked a bit too similar, but you can argue with the fact that it's the same ship, so it's not too bad. If we had sprayed it a different color, I might have been happier.

I noticed some of the tubing had the word Lister on it.

Bibby: That was the manufacturer; it's just a coincidence, Lister Manufacturing or whatever. That particular set was left to Vendetta to make. I did a sketch of what we needed, where we needed the cupboards, and Vendetta dressed it. They're a special FX company across the road, run Jim Francis, who I've known for many years. We tend to use them for any kind of special prop-making or small sets like that. While Dave Green would do the major construction like the saloon, Jim's boys would do the small stuff.

With the 'Legion' set, I notice visual FX duplicated your set into their model.

Bibby: That's the advantage of doing the model shots later, because the boys can pick up what the studio sets or the location stuff is like, and carry that into the models.

What did you have to do on location for 'Emohawk' to coordinate what was being seen in the studio?

Bibby: We used flambeaux and fires. It was all shot at night, so the detail was going to be lost. We were still going for a medieval look, because the idea was it's a bit like a medieval culture, but they spend a lot of time trading with other civilizations, so for instance, they might be dressed in medieval costumes and living in medieval huts, but they might also be carrying space age weapons, or even a laptop computer slung over their shoulder, while their culture is still stone age. It looks a bit like Star Wars; you've got these big, monstrous medieval looking person, but he wears high-tech equipment and modern weapons, so it's that mixture of cultures.

How id you decide on the artwork used in the 'Legion' set?

Steve Bradshaw (assistant designer): With the smaller, hand-held props that have to made, it's left up to Springer to get them. He will liaise with Mel and say, 'I'm getting this...' Mel will be aware of the action of the props, and unless he wants to specifically say, 'I want these plates or whatever...'

Bibby: Springer found the big painting at the back which he brought in photos of, and it was fine by me, it was fine by Andy, so that decision was made. The sculptures were made by Effects because they had to be breakaway. The really nice ones came from a hire company, and some of the paintings that we actually used were made by an artist and thrown away afterwards. In fact, the one that was at the end of the table is now over Craig's bed. He liked it so much, he bought the painting.

Was there an effort made to make the features of the sets functional?

Bibby: Obviously a lot of it is dressing, but wherever there's a key panel that's scripted, we'll put in a working key panel. If you've seen a door without a panel, and the next week you see a door with a panel, we'll go with along with that. Red Dwarf is not an exact science; it's more suck it and see. That means that if you can't find it, if you can't make a decision, then you suck it and see what happens. It's a collective collaboration between a lot of departments, and whatever they need eventually gets done.

Howard Burden (Costume Designer)

What was your brief for season six?

Howard Burden: We were told that we are now 200 years in the future, so it seemed like the ideal opportunity to revamp the whole look for all of them. I talked to Rob and Doug, and we decided that we wanted Lister away from the biker leather look, giving him more of a space look. We had some initial questions about Cat; even though he's left Red Dwarf in a hurry, my argument was he'd still have time to pack something, but we streamlined him a lot. He's basically in the same outfit, with a few changes he's managed to squirrel away, but without the full Monty

With Kryten, we decided that he's managed to re-vamp and rejuvenate himself over the years, so he's a lot more high-tech. It was primarily to give him more comfort in wearing the costume, because with that and the head, it's so unbearable, so this gave him a lot more flexibility; Kryten's doing a lot more physically, so we had to give him optimum movement for that. It's a clean slate with him.

For Chris, it seemed sensible that if we changed the other two characters and Cat is perennially changing, that he should also have a new look. It's got that same combat/military feel to it, but with more of a sci-fi look. We never actually used it, but on his belt he's got a Space Corps directive manual computer which at one stage he was going to actually remove and punch up Space Corps Directive blah blah blah. He's gotten more American I suppose, in his uniform, but they've all had to change, so we've gone along with the flow of that.

With 'Psirens,' you had quite a lot of new characters like Pete Tranter's sister and Professor Mamet. Were those costumes individually designed, or was it a matter of seeing what sort of spare bits you could put together?

Burden: They were all new. From the onset of any series of Red Dwarf, I'm given a certain budget, and within those constraints, I have to design for each episode. Obviously if the scripts are late, you have to improvise very quickly, but in the first episode we had a lot of time, so each character was well thought-out and designed on paper.

For a first episode it was quite busy, but everyone had a distinctive proper look, so Jenny Agutter as Mamet was designed with a proper fitting; the same with Pete Tranter's sister, the two sirens; they all had a distinctive look and we had the proper time to do them.

Were you trying to use different influences for some of the characters? I thought you were trying to use an Aliens look for Kochanski and Captain Tau for example.

Burden: Yes, to a certain extent, but it's not a conscious one. They're on screen for such a short time and visually you have a very short time to make an impact, and the fact that those two characters were fighting on the ship, we decided to give it a guerilla warfare look like Aliens.

What about Richard Ridings as the Mad Astro?

Burden: Because we only saw him on the monitor, we had to show that he was a futuristic character that had elements of a space outfit about him, so we decided to go with bits and pieces on the shoulders and the neck. It's not based on anything in particular, but he needed a space look, and he's mad, he's off the wall, and in that light, the black and the silver shone out on all the metal braid.

What about Pete Tranter's sister?

Burden: She's your Barbarella, Lister's dream fantasy woman, so we emphasized the breast panel and thigh boots. She was a sexy lady.

Your department did the cube Kryten?

Burden: We were trying to work out if it should be done as a computer graphic, but the boys felt it would be funnier for Robert to be in the cube. We had a lot of physical problems, getting Robert as small as possible and still be able to move, as well as making it as light as possible. We were filming on that grid floor, which was quite slippery with the tread on his boots, so it was quite difficult for him.

What did you have in mind for Legion?

Burden: I was nervous about it, but I love the mask, which is so serene, which was just what I needed, because when the mask comes away and he's a metamorphosis of the four of them, that's when it turns horrible. The mask had almost a friendly quality to it to start with.

I decided that the tube was part of a regeneration, that when he fed, it kept the body warm and full of nutrients, so rather than someone just wearing a mask, it also had a slight medical quality with those tubes and wires, which was slightly sinister.

We also introduced the hard light Rimmer, which has obviously made things much easier in subsequent programs now that he could touch things. It was a matter of getting that two-toned fabric that works well on camera, and you get that sort of shimmer, and I think the blue looks very good on camera.

With 'Rimmerworld,' were you trying to mesh certain periods with the costumes?

Burden: Not consciously, no. The brief was that it was Romanesque/medieval, a lot of mixed cultures within the set, and I felt the Roman period was great for Rimmerworld, that whole Emperor-dominated world. From a comedy point of view, Rimmer in a Roman Legion outfit with an Emperor's helmet; that was comedy in itself. The two handmaidens were a concoction of making them gorgeous and leading up to that screen kiss and I think it worked very well.

What did you want to do with Liz as the simulant?

Burden: Obviously we couldn't afford to do two complete outfits, one of them after she's left the ship, it's burnt out and destroyed, so we had to take the basic outfit and adds bits which we could then remove comfortably for the following week when she had to be clean. We made her lose her arm, so she had to wear her own arm strapped to her back, so it was a case of, "What can we do to achieve this without getting into fantastic expense?'

I would imagine that **'Gunmen'** was the episode where all your money got spent.

Burden: To a certain extent, it was easier in that it was a cowboy episode, and the brief we had was that they should be as realistic as possible. We weren't creating a whole new realm of cowboys, but the boys needed an identity that was right for each character. With Danny as the Riviera Kid, we toyed with The Rhinestone Cowboy to start with, and came up with the Spanish/Mexican embroidered jacket. It retained the elements of Cat within the reality of shooting that scene.

Did you have to design all of the costumes, or just seeing what was available?

Burden: They were all hired. We don't have the funds to have a new set of cowboy duds made, or the time to get outfits that had to be broken down and made more realistic. We went to specialists who dealt specifically with cowboy outfits, and I carefully went through each item of clothing I wanted for each character. With Famine and Death, we kept them dark and sinister, but obviously with Famine we decided to make him fat, so things come through very fast, and you have to make them up as you go along.

I presume you did the same thing with the gangster costumes in the opening?

Burden: They were hired. We had the practicality of trying to find hats big enough to fit over Kryten' s mask- whenever you put anything over his head, you take the risk that you might rip it and lose a day's shoot or three or four hours while they redo his head. Because we were going to shoot that it in sepia, I wanted it to have an authentic Humphrey Bogart look, so a lot of the clothes were original 40's clothing I got from a hire company. And to get that Hollywood gangster look, particularly with the girl, we had some contemporary elements that we used on her, but essentially it was to get it as realistic as possible.

That brings us to 'Emohawk.' I assume you weren't expecting the amount of work that would have to be done with the GELFs.

Burden: They were a surprise (laughs). We had less than a week's time, because we had to have them ready by the Thursday, and we were given the script on the previous Tuesday. It was an attempt to put together something that looked grisly and warty and Yeti-like, but with artistic license, and I was really pleased with the way they did look. Makeup found these latex masks, and we used a basic body stocking to cover the flesh, as well as plumber's hemp, which is the stuff they clean the pipes with. It has that smell to it which you'll have noticed if you've stood beside them, which I thought was quite funny. It just added to the fact that they were so disgusting. It was cheap but effective, and I think that comes from having a degree in theatre design, where you do use elements of whatever you have within the limited budget. I suppose if we had lot lots of money, I would have used hair, and they would have been fully covered, but it works and that's what we did.

With Dwayne, you used the costume from last season?

Burden: He was established last year, and it was every element that was anti-Cat, anti-style, anti-taste, so he's in a nylon shirt, ghastly polyester trousers and a rancid anorak; it's just tasteless and it works very well. I think Danny comes alive when he does Dwayne. He gets very animated, and he's very funny. We did an episode in series three where he lost his cool and became a tramp. His hair was all matted, and that in itself was funny, just to see that change.

What sort of problems are you coming up against with the final episode?

Burden: The biggest problem is we've got three days to put them all together. Each character has a completely new look, as they're all fatter and older. Rimmer's in a new color, Danny has a paunch; he's had too much of a good time, and Kryten is an oversize jacket, turtleneck and toupee, trying to look as human as possible. Lister, in the one page I've seen, has a robot body, with a glass sphere on top of his head where his brain sits in this liquid, so we've got to create an entire robot costume, and we have to do that in three days. The only thing in our favor is that it should look hammy; it shouldn't look like a superb robot.

What have you been happiest with this series so far?

Burden: I think Kryten looks terrific. I saw an episode from series five episode last night, and Kryten looked quite cumbersome. I like the look now, which is more high-tech and suits him very well. The coloring of the fabric is terrific, and the actual detail on it is enough but not too much. He's got a lot more flexibility and Robert is a lot happier as an actor, so that's worked very well.

On the whole, I think Craig looks good. I'm pleased we got away from the biker leather. I'm pleased with the look of most of the boys, because it was a chance to have something fresh and new, and you always try to bring something innovative and exciting into the program. If we went from series to series with the same costumes, it would begin to look quite tired.

Andria Pennell (Makeup)

Let's start by talking about how the characters have changed from last season. What have you done to Kryten, for example?

Andria Pennell: Kryten has been remodeled, but he's stayed basically the same. There's a slight difference because it's a different sculptor, but in theory, he's supposed to look the same every year. I suppose the big difference is the mouth, which was made wider. The eyes unfortunately, should have been further away from Robert's own eyes, but they're not, so that's another thing we'll have to try and do next time. There was also a big campaign, certainly on Robert's behalf, to have the mask from the American pilot, where he had his mouth free, because it makes such a difference to have it in pieces, but unfortunately they wanted the original mask.

What about the other characters?

Pennell: They've basically stayed the same. There are changes or modifications in costume, but makeup-wise they wanted them to look the same from the neck upwards.

With 'Psirens,' your first responsibility was putting the wig, beard and nails on Craig?

Pennell They wanted seven-inch nails for his fingers and toes, and a beard made, so we had to put the whole ensemble together. Craig isn't the easiest person to put the stuff on, so it's best really, to have doubles ready for him.

For 'Legion,' did you have to create the combination face on Nigel?

Pennell: Not really, that was literally just in case you saw his face if he turned, Andy wanted some sort of makeup that would match the computer effect, so we used Rimmer's 'H,' a quarter of Kryten and then painted Craig and Danny's skin colors and then Cat's teeth. From the way it was shot, you don't see any of it.

What did you do in 'Rimmerworld' to make Chris more feminine?

Pennell: He looked quite good as a girl; not quite Tootsie, but base, mascara, a bit of eye shadow and the lips. It was good fun.

'Gunmen' was a big episode, starting with the four Horsemen.

Pennell: On Pestilence, we built up some latex built up and plastic pieces, which worked quite well. I was disappointed that you couldn't see more of it, because a lot of work that went into it. Famine had a lot of shading to make him look as fat as possible. With War, we dirtied him down; and Denis as Death had stubble put on and aged. His teeth were blacked out and nicotined.

What about Denis as the Rogue Simulant?

Pennell: We tried to give him a waxy look, so we put quite a thick base on and let it go shiny, so he would a sort of plasticized look about it. Double eyebrows again, and that was it, really. The thing is, he wouldn't take the moustache off, so it all got to be too much with eyebrows and moustache.

Did they cast cowboys with facial hair, or did you have to put beards and moustaches on them?

Pennell: They pretty much cast the right people. We put sideboards on, and beards and stubble, but the extras people in Laredo were great.

For the gangster scene, did you research 1920s makeup and how it was going to look in black and white?

Lois Burwell: It involved contrasty shading, but we know that anyway. We're hen trained to do these things.

Pennell: And that era is quite contrasty anyway- the face, the lips.

Burwell: If it was on film rather than on video, and you wanted to do an absolute replica of a film noir type movie like Double Indemnity, then you would change the color tone, because they did have different color tones then.

With 'Emohawk,' was that mainly a matter of digging out Danny and Chris's wigs?

Pennell: Yes, but again, Chris's wig was lost, so this is a modified version. And Danny's teeth as well from the last series, which are like a brace that literally clips over his teeth just like a brace.

What did you do with the GELFs?

Pennell: The GELFs were literally somebody's test pieces, learning how to do prosthetics. We didn't have the budget to do any prosthetics, but the guy who does Kryten's mask for us said, "Oh, I've got this old monkey mold," so he sent it over. I had a chat with Lois, who suggested cutting out the chin, which was the one thing that didn't fit the rest of the face, so we cut the chin out, and then dug into Lois's beard box and found something that would cover up the chin part. I had to lay on the hair over it, so you wouldn't know it was a piece that had been chopped about, and then warts and scabby bits put on.

How did you decide what you were going to do in the final episode?

Pennell: They were supposed to be meeting themselves from the future, so of them had to be fat and aged, but I said that Danny wouldn't be that fat for his age, really.

I understood Danny's future was going to be bald?

Pennell: It wasn't that funny. We wanted to find funnier for him because he didn't have that many funny lines. He had all the feed lines, but not that many funny lines. Chris had all the funny lines, so his hair was like his own, only grey.

And Robert's toupee?

Pennell: That was supposed to be funny. It was supposed to be like Tom Jones, rather than something like a crash helmet. Also, we wanted something with a bit of movement to it.

How much aging was being done on Danny and Chris?

Pennell: The thing is, if they're supposed to be graying and debauched, it can't be 15 years, so we had do more, maybe 20; otherwise it just wouldn't be that funny if they were just grey around the temples.

So what have you been happiest with this series?

Pennell: With the GELFS, actually. Pleasantly surprised.

And least happy?

Pennell: I wish we could have done more with the simulants. I didn't like the way Denis looked either with the moustache, so that's probably my biggest disappointment.

Graham Hutchings (Editor)

Let's start by talking about what your job entails.

Graham Hutchings: I am involved at a very early stage, looking at scripts with Andy or whoever is directing and Rob and Doug at the early stages, to get a clear idea of what's involved in terms of effects and things that might affect the final product in terms of editing. We go through the script to decide what can and can't be done, and if there's anything that's particularly difficult, we consult the effects people or try to work our way around it. That's the first stage.

Having sorted most of those problems out, I invariably come to the studio to make sure everything's okay; anticipating any potential editing problems that might arise from pickups, or anything that goes on in the studio. The director is obviously looking at all sorts of things on the night, and can't particularly concentrate on what problems might arise from the editing, so with me there, he has the confidence of knowing that if he walks away, everything is more or less covered.

The next stage is on the Monday following the studios. I do a rough assembly, which is basically to get everything in story order, and cut together all the preferred takes that we've marked up on the studio night. That's mainly in order to get an idea that everything has worked and to see if there are any flaws in what we've got. Andy, Rob, Doug and I then look at those tapes and decide if we need to do any further pickups or re-shoots to get all the material in the can. At the end of the series, there's always one major pickup day simply to cover shots that didn't work, or any problems. It's certainly it's the most complex show on British television as far as dealing with conceptually difficult ideas, as well as well-written comedy material, plus the effects as well.

The next process is to do a rough cut of the shows. Andy, Chrissie the production assistant, the effects people, the models people, Rob and Doug and I sit down for four days, looking at rushes and our rough assemblies. Having looked at the rough assemblies, we would go back and look at particular takes to see if there was a different or better performance or a better laugh and make notes as to what we expected at each point in the story line.

At the same time, as each particular model shot came up, we may find there are scripted model shots and you need a shot that was unscripted in order to embellish the story line. We would talk to Peter Wragg and say, "It would be nice if we could have another model shot to depict this," and depending on the budgetary situation, you would either get another model shot or not.

In the next stage, the effects people are aware of what they need to do, so Andy and I will go away and rough-cut the first show based on these notes. We might have to brief the effects people or re-brief Peter Wragg, because it's a very fluid situation, so when you start editing the thing together tightly, these problems can start to materialize.

The next process is to do a fine cut from the rough cut, because the show may still be over-length at this point. We can get most of that time down at the rough-cut stage to about a minute over, just by tightening the performance. Virtually no breath of dialogue is left untouched, although we try and protect all the laughs we can get. At the fine cut stage, we're still maybe a minute to a minute 30 seconds over, and it's a fairly easy process to get that out. It's not generally a problem, because you've got some elasticity in the model shots, so you can cut the odd second out and gain 30 seconds fairly easily.

The next stage is to bring all the various elements together. At this stage, the effects are still being processed, so you have to imagine how these effects are going to be. They basically get a tape from us with the programs cut to length now, and they paint effects where they can on top of the shots I've provided them. A lot of the model shots I make up myself from various elements of live action, and blue screen shots of Starbug that I have here, so a lot of the shots you see in the final product are a mixture of Peter Wragg's stuff, live action, and a bit of nebula that I composite in the on-line suite. From the various elements that Peter gives me, I can make up maybe another 5-6 shots.

After the final on-line where we've got it all to length with all the shots in, it goes to the BBC and gets dubbed, which is Keith's job, and the music is put in, and it comes back here again where we put the final credits on. The last bit we do is to cut the opening titles using shots out of the various shows.

How closely do Rob, Doug and Andy get involved in the process?

Hutchings: Very closely. Rob and Doug less so this time, because they've been off writing their book, so they've not been around as much as they have the past two series. But that's been a conscious decision on their part to do that, to keep their hands on the tiller, but relinquish the earlier responsibilities of having to be here for the rough cut. They don't come for the assemblies of the shows, but they do come for the last tweaks. Obviously we get notes from them all the time, but I think they're so busy they physically don't have the time to be here anymore.

How much work goes into Red Dwarf compared to everything else, and how much do you enjoy it for its entertainment value?

Hutchings: It's undoubtedly the best program I work on in the year without a doubt. From a written point of view, It's the most intelligent form of comedy I've ever worked on, and I've known Rob and Doug for a long time, and I admire the way they write, but creatively, there's nothing else on British television that comes anywhere near it. From an editor's point of view, it's a dream.

And also, you know the show is going to get 6-7 million viewers too, and the figures are going up. It's such a cult thing, but at the end of the day, it's what's on the screen that you know is making that.

Howard Goodall (Composer)

At what point in the program do you actually come into it?

Howard Goodall: The incidental music within each program and within each series happens only after it's all done in the post-production stage. With this series, for example, I come in between the fine cut, the mix of sound and the sound effects and the music. The reason I come in after the fine cut is I need to work to something precisely cut, because I then synchronize it all up and precisely to picture, frame by frame. There's no point in my working to a rough cut if it's all going to change once I've started putting music onto it.

The time between final cut and the mix is usually about a week. I get the tape of the program, and then have about a week to set music to it, record it and get it to them so they can mix it in with all the other sound effects at the final mix.

So it's a given that this is a rushed process for you?

Howard: Yes (laughing), I think most composers are used to the fact that the amount of time you get is very limited, so I would generally be working nights and days to get this done in time by the very end of the process. One part of me likes the deadline, because it's very fresh in your mind and for a few days, you're thinking of nothing else and it's quite exciting trying to meet a deadline.

On the other hand, you have very little room to maneuver. If I do some music for an episode and Rob and Doug think it's not quite right, you've got almost no time left to change it, but we're now in the sixth series, and I think they generally know I'm not going to get their ideas completely wrong. Different episodes require different approaches anyway.

One of the episodes in this series has a Western theme in it, so they obviously wanted a score that would be like a western pastiche. And at the end of the episode, instead of going into our normal music for the final closing titles, we would go into a big western theme that fitted that program. They would normally give me advance warning while they're cutting it, and say, 'We're doing this one with a western theme,' so when that episode finally came to my office, I was already prepared for it.

So for different episodes, you would have a different approach for each of them.

Goodall: Exactly, and I would treat the themes, music and style differently. With 'Psirens,' we decided there would be a Psirens-type of weirdo sound when they attacked, so you got a ghostly, wailing-type noise, when they came around.

What did you do with 'Legion?'

Goodall: I haven't started on 'Legion' yet. I've got two more to do- 'Present from the Future' and 'Legion' still to do this week. I find the mixing process quite brutal with comedy. If you were doing a film, you'd probably favor the action, excitement and the visual side, and the dialogue would fight to be there, whereas when you're doing a comedy on TV, it's very important that the jokes are heard, therefore it would always favor the dialogue.

For 'Rimmerworld,' I gave them an exotic gong type sound for Rimmerworld, a sort of Romanesque musical sound as well as some drums and things. I thought 'Rimmerworld' was a very funny episode, very clever and when he goes to the planet for the first time,

I did a kind of Robinson Crusoe idea, with storm sequences and the Garden of Eden; I set all of that to music, that whole section.

There were one or two things they asked for ahead of time. They wanted the piano music in the western saloon before, because that's the Red Dwarf theme being played on a honky tonk piano, and they wanted that ahead of time so they could have it in the scene. I also did some big western themes for that one, great, epic, going off into the sunset type of things, and at the end of that episode, the western theme I developed throughout the program takes over in the final credits.

'Emohawk' had a lot of exciting action stuff at the beginning with the spaceships being chased, so I did quite a modern thing for that, quite a lot of throbbing, pulsing stuff to provide the excitement. On the planet, I went for lots of drums and strange native sounds for the camp, and there's a chase sequence where I had the drums again. Back in the ship, there's a lot of alien, looking-for-the-Emohawk low throbs. The thing I do the most in Red Dwarf is a low throb. There are so many scenes where there's a bit of tension, or they're walking around the ship. In the sixth series, I must have done more of them than anything else.

How happy are you with this series as opposed to previous ones?

Goodall: I get the feeling, and I could be wrong about this, that Rob and Doug have liked what I've been doing on this series more than previously. That's partly because 'Gunmen' and 'Rimmerworld' had such fun ideas to work on. There have been so many series now, that I feel there are cues in certain episodes that I like a lot, and certain episodes that gave me something to do. I look at it selfishly I suppose; I think there are some that give me an opportunity and some that don't.

What is it about Red Dwarf that makes it interesting to do every year?

Goodall: I think partly that I find Rob and Doug's imaginations in terms of their plots intriguing. Whenever a new series comes on, you always think, 'What are they going to come up with this time?'

They're very imaginative, so you don't know what's going to happen next. You couldn't predict there was going to be an episode set in the Wild West for example. That's the fun of it, that it's so unpredictable.

John Pomphrey (Lighting Director)

How did you collaborate with Andy on season six?

John Pomphrey: Andy, I've never met before. We had a chat at the beginning, and he's a bit of a photographer as well. He knows pictures, and he's got a good visual eye. He said he likes light and shade, and lots of dark corners and that sort of stuff, and he wanted to have more of a filmic look. We've gotten even further this series from sitcom lighting, and we are allowing people to say humorous lines not in total darkness but maybe semi-darkness. It looks more like a film, but that again is no problem at all. In the end, I'm a frustrated...I want to make Aliens. I'm a frustrated film lighter; I'd love to make a straightforward SF film. All the way down the line, I've been indulged. I've been able to move along to what we've got now, which is where I've wanted to go, and it suited everyone.

What do you think has turned out the best in this series as far as what you've been trying to do over the last few years?

Pomphrey: Color and lighting-wise? I like the cockpit and the Starbug rear more than I did before. In show one, we were still getting it right, but we've gotten a lot of depth in it now. It's big, without looking huge. There's space for movement, they can go down stairs, they can go into airlocks, they can actually walk around and it can look different just by walking across the set. I've been able to give it a different look totally, from going from Starbug front to Starbug rear and up the staircase. What sets it off nicely is the kitchen leading off it, which is a fairly high key area. Everywhere else is low key and dark and quite scruffy, and suddenly you've got this high-key, clinical type area. It sets it off. When you see it in the back of the shot, it helps you read the low key is pointed out by the fact that you've got this high key cubicle off it, so I like that area.

What would you have liked to change if given more time this series?

Pomphrey: Well, I'm getting the chance. In the engine room, in the back, it didn't work as well as it should have done, for the simulant scene. We had run out of time, and we were up against the clock and we went over while we were shooting it, but fortunately, we're doing it again, which is great. That was the only one I was really unhappy with. It was okay, but I know in my heart of hearts I could have done it better. It was almost the first time we were in there, and the trouble is, it's such a small area that two guys with booms and four cameras, we're really pushed for space, and I had to learn very quickly how all the various disciplines- sound, lighting, camera could all work together in this rather small area to get the right effect, and I've modified it slightly, putting in some extra lighting and cable, and when we do the retake, it will look a lot better. I've learned from going in there. Before we did it, we had the tech run, we don't have cameras in there, so you don't know where the cameras are physically going to go, because the tech run is fairly loose, and quite often, there's no representative from sound there, so I'm not sure how they'll cover it. I now know where the sound guys will go, having been in there a couple of times, and I know the areas they need to go in order to get the sound out of it, so I now know where I can go. I have to be sympathetic, because I could stick my nose in and say, "My lights are here, and I'm going to light it in this way," but you don't have time for that. You really have to work together, under the constraints of multi-camera shooting.

How do you think the interiors matched up with the locations? I'm thinking in particular of the Legion stuff shot in the Marco Polo Building, and the Laredo stuff.

Pomphrey: The Marco Polo stuff will match up very well, because they're going to be electronically... I chose the same colors, and we went to the location first obviously, and the construction of the building decided lots of things. I spoke to Andy, and we had a chat beforehand about the style- high-key, high-tech, and I know he's going to doctor the pictures electronically to match, and then when Mel came in the studio, he built it to match, and I deliberately chose the same colors to reflect what we had already done, and lit it in a similar way; lots of soft lights. I wanted to do it in a different style, so there was no harsh shadowy lighting at all. The location was also done completely with bounced lights, and that was the style we wanted. It gave us a different feel, so that worked well.

I was very impressed with the way the Laredo material cut together.

Pomphrey: It's got to feel the same. The viewer should never feel he's been taken somewhere else. He shouldn't be conscious of location, studio, exterior; it should all flow. If they're conscious of it, then I've failed. Nobody should be looking at the lighting, they shouldn't even be aware of it. It should match the mood of the picture, of the mood that's going on, and they shouldn't be aware of it. This isn't part of the show; it's there to enhance, to set the environment for the artist to work in. It should all sit comfortably together. If someone looks at the lighting, then I've actually failed, because I've upstaged the artists.

I decided right from the outset after speaking to Mel, how they would match up. When we were shooting the street scenes on the outside, I had put in all the little houses lamps that had rather orangy and straw gels on them to show warm colored lights coming out of the various buildings, and that created an environment for the studio stuff, which was lit in warm tones, and the final shot we took of Laredo where we panned down and saw the figures walking in, I wanted that shot, because I could then match that shot to them walking into the studio, so you got a nice flow straight through. I took my lamps with me and colored them up in such a way that it would give me- I decided how I would light the studio, and then I made the location look the same, because in the studio, you had a lot of close-ups, and I want to get myself stuck in a situation where I couldn't do it, so I had to make sure the implied interiors once we were on location would be okay, and would cut together with the real interiors once we were in the studio. There's a problem with size- invariably the cameramen use wide angle lenses and they go in close, but certainly color-wise, I don't think there's a clash at all. We did the best we could. The ideal thing would have been to build on location a frontage to match the studio set, which on a film we could have done, and probably sold it to them at the end of the day, and they would have been very happy with it.

How do you think some of the exteriors turned out, such as the woodlands scenes, or the Roman soldier scene?

Pomphrey: I asked Andy what he wanted beforehand, and a director always wants to keep his options open, so when he edits, he can adjust the tints and the hues on the location stuff, but fortunately with the Rimmerworld stuff, we never saw any exteriors of buildings, so as long as it feels the same, it should look all right.

What about the village shot at night?

Pomphrey: Same decision, really. We went down and looked at the huts, and I did exactly the same as we did at Laredo: I put oranges and straw-colored gels in the huts, which would carry me through to the huts in the studio. I tend to work backwards in these ways, so I spoke to Mel and looked at the design for the huts and we talked about it. The dialogue was in the street, so that was okay; there was no dialogue in any of the interiors, so all the dialogue was in the street, which was lit with flambeaux, so I carried through the flambeau lighting, and lit the interiors with straws and oranges so they appeared to be lit with flames. I'd made the decision before we went on location how I would light the interiors. I knew there was a fire, so I wanted to light it as if it were from a fire, and used warm lights on the floor to beef up the fire itself, and I beefed it up with small lamps lighting people from the floor, so it looked like it was coming from the fire, and I gave it a depth of separation by putting blue nighttime lighting through the windows just to pick up the sides of their faces. I then worked backwards from there and used big lamps with blue gels on them to light the village, and then orange and straw lamps again to light the close-ups as if the light was spilling from doorways. Then when they went into the woods, I just lit them with blue lights as if they were away from the village, so I didn't put any warm colored lighting on them at all, so I lit them with different shades of blue. I spoke to Mike the visual engineer, who adjusted the colors anyway to suit the scene. He can change the colors as well. He's got the ability, so we decided the woods would look a certain color.

SVC (Video Effects)

Let's start with 'Psirens' and the light bee sequence for that episode.

Carl Mooney: They edited that screen graphic into the show and sent over some clean backgrounds where Rimmer in real life on the set would be materializing, and I did about three shots for that so we were cutting back and forth between the screen graphic and the shot of him actually materializing. I did a bit of a 3D particle system which was basically like TV noise or fizz- which I pinched from another job actually- which was a particle system swirling its way around the figure as it was materializing, and I brought some of the colors through from the graphic onto the character as each characteristic was actually brought into the character: arrogance, charisma, etc.

For all the shooting shots- and there were quite a few of them in that program, there was the Anita Dobson sequence where there was lots of firing, and then we shot the monster and things like that- I used some new 3D software called Paint Effects every time someone was firing a gun or being shot. I did the laser beams, flashes from the end of a gun, and reflections on the bodies as the guns fired. Each time a laser would pass someone firing, I put little reflections on the person as well. A couple of scenes were really improved by that.

What about 'Legion?'

Mooney: On 'Legion,' there were two shots of the comet Legion flying around before it he'd grabbed Starbug, so I produced the comet in 3D. I just had a b/w matte done, and then put color into that, and had a bubble made up with what would most probably be described as a slinky behind it, which came out from the model shoot of the space station. It envelopes Starbug and pulls it into the ship, for which I did four or five 5 shots. I created a wire frame bubble in 3D and put some glowing edges around it, so it was like a slinky joined that bubble to Legion's space station, and it actually looked quite nice, that bubble around it.

Have you finished the big morphing sequence yet?

Mooney: That's the one I've left until tonight. I could have spent the whole time just working on those faces, so I thought I've got to get all the other stuff out of the way before I do that. I could go on playing with them forever, but I've done eight or so tests of what they could look like in different combinations of the four characters on the face, and they've sort of picked one, which is Rimmer's forehead and nose, and then Kryten and Lister- an eye each and Cat's mouth. It's pretty much what I did for the original tests, but there's and it looks quite convincing.

What about the dinner sequence?

Mooney: That could easily have another week's work on it. I've put a particle system fizz around the chopsticks with a slight glow around them, and that basically took me a day and all night and half the next day to actually do it. The reason it took so long is because you have to track it. Obviously they wave those chopsticks about and there wasn't a single frame where the chopstick was in the same position, so I had to track them and put the fizz on the end, a bit like putting a laser on the end of Luke Skywalker's light saber, so it just took ages. I think if I had another day on it, I could really improve it, but what I've done so far helps it anyway. It's a massive task to save something like that; none of that food looked edible in the slightest.

Did you have a lot of work on 'Gunmen?'

Mooney: For the virus, I ran the live action sequence through Paint Effects, and what I wanted was for that character to have the virus for the whole time, but Rob and Doug thought it was more important that it actually looked like it entered him, and was within him rather than on the outside. In the end, I did two or three shots of the virus entering Kryten with an organic wipe as he was jerking around, and that sequence worked quite well.

When Kryten throws the doves at them in the end, I put that same virus inside the cowboys as they collapse when Kryten zaps them. I did a small morph for when Kryten pulls out his handguns, and they changed into the doves, which was quite a tricky one because at no point in the sequence they had with the doves and the guns, he obviously threw the guns out once and then threw the doves out, so there was only one point where they were anywhere near being close to each other in order to do the morph. That happened to be just as he was pulling them out of the actual holster, so we were tied to where we could actually do the morph.

I did the flies in 3D as a particle system, and we had five little black circles that we ran through 3D. It's a very quick shot; only about 25 frames or so. There were also a few gunshots which I treated the same way, so I put the little flashes on where Cat fires the bullets in the saloon. For the whip, I painted in frame by frame. It had to actually wrap itself around the bottle before it was jerked out, so it was around a second and half on Paint Box just to paint that in. They didn't have the right kind of shot when they came to cut it, because the whip had to come in a lot earlier. Actually painting it in, it looked really convincing, but when you cut to the next shot, it does spoil it a bit because it swings back in.

That brings us to the final three episodes.

Mooney: For 'Rimmerworld,' I had to do a composite shot of Starbug coming out of the exploding skull. I also did about eight teleporting sequences using a bit of 3D texture to do a Star Trek-type teleporting. We also produced a wormhole in 3D, something similar to the movie The Black Hole that they went into, and they comped the ship on top of it. That was the escape pod, and Starbug eventually goes in after him. It was quite a nice sequence and it's a shame it was squashed because it looked really powerful when it filled up the screen.

With 'Emohawk,' I enhanced the explosion where Rimmer falls on the grenade, using some live-action explosions, plus some 3D, and then there were all the morphs. There were about 12 morphs of the Emohawk changing from table lamp to chicken to a tin of beans, and again, I used some Paint Effects frames and some fizz just before the morph happened, which signaled the morph. I was hoping they were going to put a little sound effect on that, and they liked the idea of a little signal that it was supposed to happen.

Unfortunately, we could only morph stills. If we had had the time, we would have done them as moving things, and that could have gotten out of hand, but in the end that was all we could do anyway.

With 'Present from the Future,' there were supposed to be a few shooting shots, and then we had to do Starbug exploding, which I think is going to be the last shot of the series. We had the live-action explosion from Peter Wragg, and I added bits in 3D just of various pieces of Starbug, a bit of a leg or fuselage, and just keyed them onto the explosion. I didn't much more of that one. They chucked the explosion on us at the last minute and said, 'Forget those other shots; can you do this explosion?' and we hardly any time to do that. We had a guy spending an entire day in 3D exploding bits and pieces.

What are you happiest with?

Mooney: Things like the use of paint effects frames that ran through 3D. We only got this bit of software a month or two ago, and it was good to use for things like the virus. I was pleased with all the shooting shots, using paint effects frames for the little reflections. The bubble around Starbug was quite nice. And playing sequence graphics; I was quite pleased with that.

Is there anything you would have liked to do, given more time?

Mooney: I think lots of scenes needed more time. With the morphing, it would have been nice to have moving shots; and things like the dinner sequence could have used another day on it. I think we generally needed more involvement in the earlier stages of the production; things changed so quickly that we never really saw clear storyboards of what the shots were going to be like. I think that was mostly because they didn't know what they were going to be like. Unless we know earlier what the stuff is going to be like, we can't get involved in saying, 'You can do something here!' We're not used to working like that, but it seemed to be the way the way everything worked. We were supposed to have a couple of months on it, but it ended up five programs being done in two weeks, and another in a week (while doing other things at the same time), so it's not like you're dedicated to doing it within that time.

...

Afterword

Although that ends my time on the Red Dwarf set, the story continued. According to my agreement with Grant Naylor Productions, I was to turn in my first draft of approximately 125 pages, which due June 1, 1993.

What I had in mind was to break the book up into sections, such as design (makeup, costume, set); technical (camera, sound, lighting); post-production (music, editing, electronic and model FX) and so on. I would then use the filming of 'Gunmen' as the example of how these departments all came together during a typical week.

In mid-June, I get a call from Doug. They like the first draft, but there are a few minor corrections they'd like to see. Such as? Well, maybe it could be cut down a bit. How much? Say...forty percent?

Needless to say, my entire first draft flew out the window. By losing 40% of my original text (which later became 50%!), there was no way to keep the original structure. One does not start building a house and then remove half its foundations.

After a few days of deliberation, I hit upon a compromise of sorts. I would have to jettison large chunks of material, but I'd keep the filming of 'Gunmen' as the focal point. I could then use interviews with the various cast and crew, but as sidebar pieces to the running narrative. Unfortunately, I'd have to lose most of their comments on the other five episodes, but at least their contribution would be there.

The idea was fine with Rob and Doug, who agreed to send me an audio tape with some additional comments on 'Gunmen' to flesh out the main section. A days later, the tape arrived, and I was able to add that information to the book. I rewrote the entire manuscript from scratch, and turned it in, in person when I returned to London a few weeks later.

More time goes by. The final book has yet to be approved by Grant Naylor, and the Penguin people are getting very nervous. The book's editor Tony Lacey asks me if I could come in and have a meeting with him. Nobby Clark the photographer, and a representative of Noel Gay (who represent Grant Naylor). We sit down to discuss a few ideas, how the book should be presented, etc. One of the art directors comes in to show us a mockup of the cover. It's a bright purple, with the words "By Rob Grant and Doug Naylor" in huge letters. My name is nowhere to be found. Because my agreement is with Grant Naylor, I don't say anything to Penguin, but I'm less than happy when Kate from Noel Gay starts volunteering me to do things like write the captions. I do suggest a few ideas, such as printing the cover in earthy, western tones, and maybe even changing the trademark Red Dwarf ellipse into a horseshoe.

As we leave the meeting, I quietly point out to Kate that my contract actually calls for my name to be on the cover (only fair, since I wrote it) and that possibly she should stop volunteering me for things that aren't in my contract until we get this matter resolved. She agrees to bring it to Rob and Doug's agent immediately.

I was going to attend the Dimension Jump convention in Manchester not long after that, and Helen, Rob and Doug's assistant called and asked if I could have breakfast with them on the Sunday morning of the convention. There were a few minor changes that still had to be made. We met up and talked over a few ideas. Instead of having a lot of sidebars, they wanted all that material to blend seamlessly into the rest of the narrative. Mind you, none of this was ever mentioned previously. Since the book had to be turned in to Penguin in a matter of days in order to meet its October release date, those changes had to be made fast We compromised by writing material to link the sidebars into the main text, and indicating where they'd have to be added. Helen would then retype the entire manuscript and send it off to Penguin after I approved it. They've also assured me that the business with the book's cover was a complete oversight, and my name would indeed be on the cover.

Several more weeks go by. At this point, I had assumed the book had been sent to Penguin long ago. Helen asks me if I would do the captions, which had to be finished within a matter of days. I was actually leaving for the States the next day, so I wasn't happy about it, especially with no warning. Nonetheless, the book was late getting to the printer, and Rob and Doug's agent made a few veiled threats about taking action if I wasn't willing to do the captions. A photo copy of the book was messengered to me before I left, and I spent most of the flight home writing captions. Within a day or so, it was sent back to Penguin.

There are two ironic endings to this story; one of them good, one not so good. Choose whichever ending you prefer. A few months later, I find out from the editor that The Making of Red Dwarf will not be released in October to coincide with season six. Apparently Rob and Doug had sat on the final manuscript for too long before giving their final approval. By the time they gave it their okay, Penguin was forced to pull it from their schedule.

On the other hand, Rob and Doug were hard at work on their third Red Dwarf novel, which by a twist of fate was not going to be published in- you guessed it- October! A cynical person might think they deliberately delayed approving my book in order to get their novel in the stores in its place, but I'm not a cynical person. At least I wasn't when this tale began.

Now here's the good ending. For whatever reason, Rob and Doug were not able to get their new novel, The Last Human, finished in time for their fall deadline. For that matter, it wasn't finished in 1994 either. As I write these words at the end of '94, Penguin still doesn't know when it will be published

On the other hand, The Making of Red Dwarf was finally released in the winter of 1994, just as Red Dwarf was in the middle of repeats on BBC2. I got a call from the publicist at Penguin telling me that it had cracked the London Times best-seller list at number eight. The book had only been in the stores for ten days. It began selling steadily, and Penguin was very happy with it. I even got to do my first book signing, at Forbidden Planet, alongside Robert

Llewellyn, whose book The Man in the Rubber Mask had been released on the same day.

When I look at that book now, I choose not to think of the numerous headaches and heartaches that went into its creation. Instead, I remember a group of wonderful people who accepted me as one of their own for two months in the winter of 1993. Those are very special memories, and nothing will ever change that. And many years later, I finally got to tell the rest of the story…

www.ingramcontent.com/pod-product-compliance
Ingram Content Group UK Ltd.
Pitfield, Milton Keynes, MK11 3LW, UK
UKHW021907190726
13853UKWH00002B/563

9 798887 715568